The Republican Party

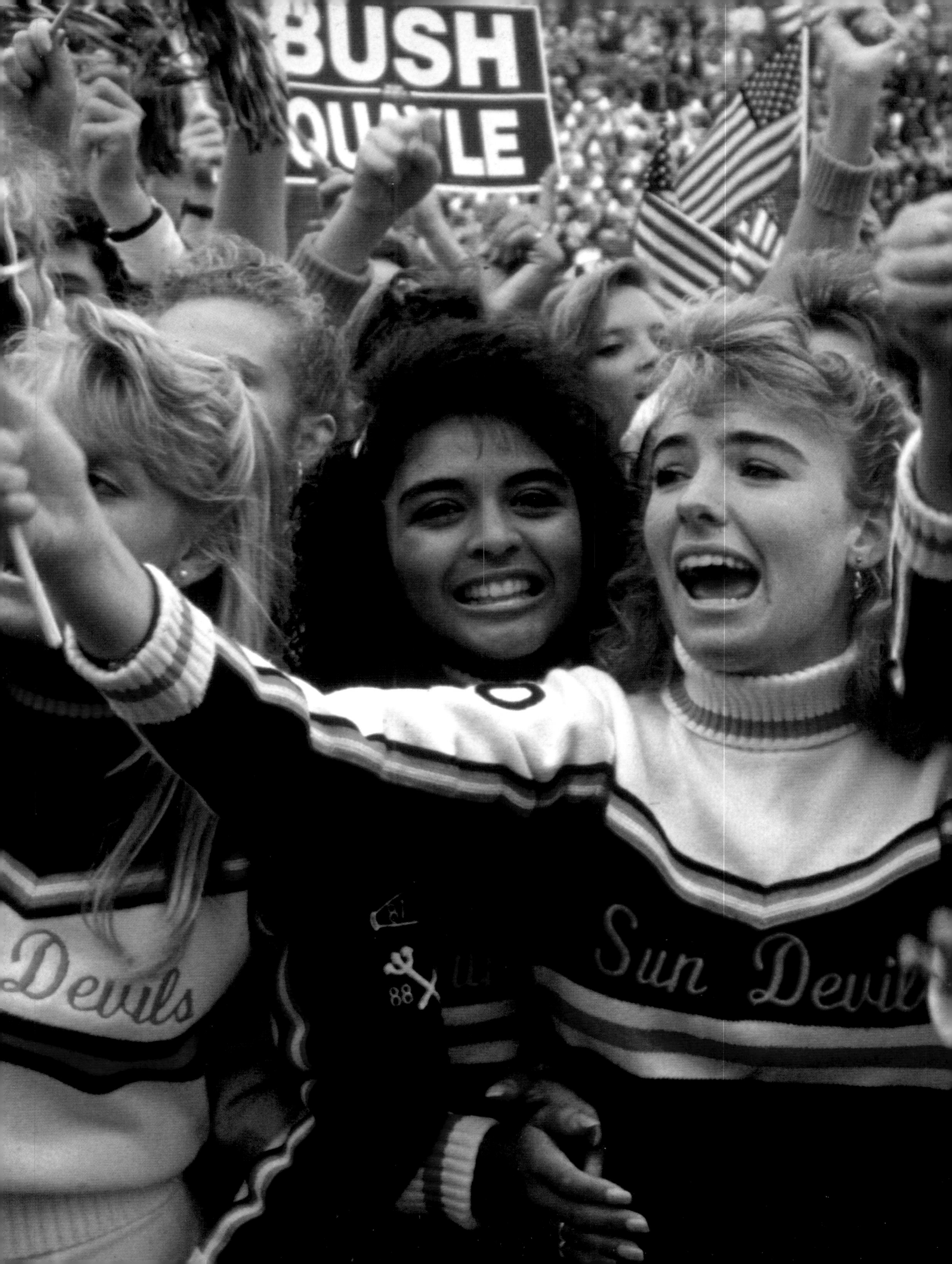
BUSH
Devils
88
Sun Devil

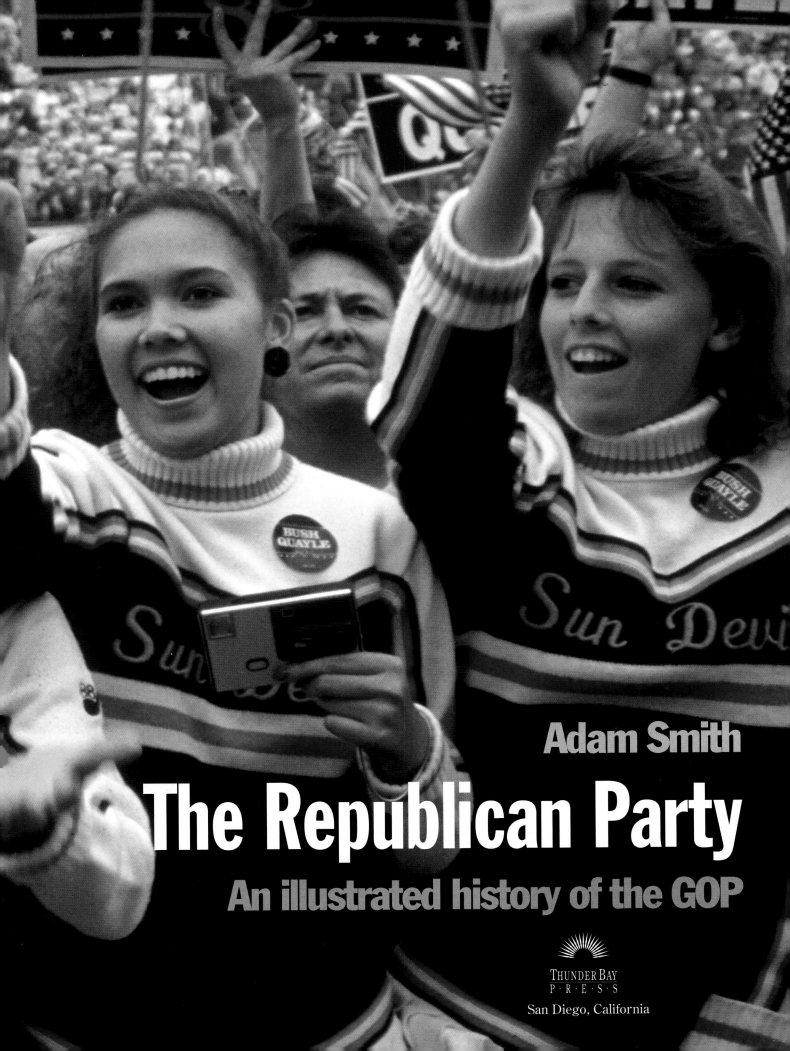

Adam Smith

The Republican Party

An illustrated history of the GOP

Thunder Bay
P · R · E · S · S

San Diego, California

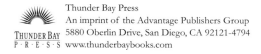

Thunder Bay Press
An imprint of the Advantage Publishers Group
5880 Oberlin Drive, San Diego, CA 92121-4794
www.thunderbaybooks.com

All notations of errors or omissions should be addressed to Thunder Bay Press, Editorial
Department, at the above address. All other correspondence (author inquiries, permissions)
concerning the content of this book should be addressed to Getty Images, 21-31 Woodfield Road,
London W9 2BA, England.

ISBN 1-59223-064-4
Library of Congress Cataloging-in-Publication Data available upon request.

Printed in Singapore
1 2 3 4 5 07 06 05 04 03

Editor: Edward Horton
Design: Paul Welti
Picture Research: Ali Khoja
Production: Mary Osborne
Special thanks: Jennifer Jeffrey, Tea McAleer, Franziska Payer Crockett,
Mia Bremridge, and Sara Green

Page 1

Four Republican heroes: Abraham Lincoln,
Theodore Roosevelt, Dwight Eisenhower,
and Ronald Reagan.

Pages 2–3

A jubilant young generation of
Republicans during the 1988 election
campaign, when their hero, President
Reagan, makes an appearance at a rally
in San Bernardino, California.

Contents

The Great Communicator: With his intuitive feel for the national mood, Ronald Reagan radiated optimism and faith in the American dream. He is seen here with his wife, Nancy, hosting a conference of GOP governors in California in 1968.

Introduction

SPEAKING TO THE REPUBLICAN National Convention in 1984, President Ronald Reagan set out what he saw as fundamental differences between Republicans and Democrats: "The choices this year are . . . between two different visions of the future, two fundamentally different ways of governing—their government of pessimism, fear, and limits, or ours of hope, confidence, and growth. Their government sees people only as members of groups, ours serves all the people of America as individuals." With these words Reagan set out the themes that would bring him one of the biggest electoral victories in American history. In 1984, with Reagan as their candidate, Republicans were entitled to feel that their values had captured the spirit and the mood of the American people.

More than 120 years earlier, Republican presidential candidate Abraham Lincoln also set out the "difference between the Republican and the Democratic Parties on the leading issue of this contest." The new Republican Party, he declared, "consider[s] slavery a moral, social, and political wrong, while [Democrats] do not consider it either a moral, social, or political wrong." Although the chattel slavery that brought the nation to the brink of destruction in the 1860s has long since been extinguished, both Lincoln and Reagan attacked their Democratic opponents as backward-looking and portrayed the Republicans as the party of the future. But what else, if anything, do these two politicians, speaking in such different circumstances, have in common? What connects the Great Communicator with the Great Emancipator? Is the Republican Party of today any longer, in any meaningful sense, the "party of Lincoln?"

American political parties are very large and often unwieldy organizations, but within their capacious ideological boundaries, some key themes provide the broad outlines of two alternative political traditions. The story of the Republican Party told in these pages is one that, when all the necessary qualifications and exceptions have been made, shows some striking continuities from Lincoln's time to ours. In particular, three ideas—individual freedom, social order, and a pride in American power—have, over a century and a half, run through the rhetoric of Republican politicians.

First, individual freedom. Ever since they pushed for the revolutionary post–Civil War constitutional amendments that abolished slavery and gave African Americans citizenship for the first time, Republicans have held fast to the principle of equality before the law. As individualists, Republicans in the nineteenth and early twentieth centuries condemned what they regarded as the "class legislation" favored by the Democrats, by which they meant legislation to protect the rights of workers to strike or attempts to provide relief for debtors. Republican individualism is based upon an unshakable certainty that the American economic system guarantees social mobility—what Lincoln called "the right to rise." Because they believe that the capitalist system rewards hard work and talent, everyone in America, they argue, can succeed on the basis of his or her own effort.

Alongside this confidence in the natural ability of the market to provide for those who work hard enough, Republicans have always been strong advocates of the idea that there is a fundamental harmony

Father Abraham: This charming image of Lincoln reading to his youngest son, Tad, sold millions of copies as an engraving.

A soldier holds up the torn flag of the Eighth Pennsylvania Reserve Color Guard. The Civil War consolidated the position of the Republican Party and provided a storehouse of memories on which it was able to draw for decades to come.

of interest among all social classes. What benefits the millionaire also benefits the ordinary working folk—or, as one Republican cabinet member once put it, what is good for General Motors is good for America. It follows that, to Republicans, all attempts to set up artificial barriers—of class or race, for example—and the claim that special consideration is due to this or that group is a violation of Reagan's golden rule that we "serve the people of America as individuals."

The second important pillar in the Republican tradition is maintaining social order. In this sense, Republicans are genuinely the party of conservatism. Protecting the family and the moral health of society is a distinctive Republican campaign pitch, one closely related to a strong tradition of evangelical Christianity. Today more than two thirds of registered Republicans describe themselves as born-again Christians—in the nation as a whole, that number falls to one in four. For these people, the Republican Party is the route to national salvation.

At the top of their agenda is outlawing abortion, but for groups like the Christian Coalition, the aim is nothing less than "Christianizing America . . . spreading the gospel in a political context." Of course not all Republicans share such zeal—campaigning in the 2000 primaries, Arizona senator John McCain attacked the Religious Right for "destroying" the Republican Party—but the tendency to conceive of politics as a moral crusade has a very long lineage in Republican Party history. As often as possible, Democrats have been associated with forces bent on destroying social order. In the closing years of the nineteenth century, Benjamin Harrison once rather unconvincingly accused Grover Cleveland—just about the most conservative opponent any Republican has ever faced—of offering no less than a "program of demolition."

This has been a familiar theme in more recent times—liberals accused of undermining the traditional values of family, patriotism, and community. Republicans have consistently presented themselves as the party of "law and order," promising to be tough on criminals. They have also been the loudest in warning of threats, conspiracies, and dangerous subversives. For Lincoln it was the "Slave Power" in the South that sought to undermine the principle of freedom. For later Republicans, it was anarchists, radicals, or Communists who were the threat. "There isn't room anywhere in these United States for anyone who preaches destruction of the government," warned presidential candidate Warren Harding in 1920 at the height of the first great Red Scare, in words that could have been spoken by any Republican at any time.

A medal commemorating an encampment of the Grand Army of the Republic at Buffalo in 1897. By keeping alive the memory of the Civil War, the GAR played a vital role in the electoral success of Republicans in the late nineteenth century.

The third pillar in the Republican pantheon is the nation. The United States, Teddy Roosevelt once said, was "the greatest republic upon which the sun has ever shone," and Richard Nixon explained that the cause of the Republican Party was "the cause of making this the greatest nation in the world, the leader of the world, because without our leadership, the world will know nothing but war, possibly starvation, or worse, in the years ahead. With our leadership it will know peace, it will know plenty." In thinking about the rest of the world, Republican thought has been characterized by a dread and a yearning. A dread of foreign threats, an anxiety about the vulnerability of American freedom in an unfriendly world, means that Republican presidents and congresses have always, in the modern era, built up the military and have been suspicious of a multilateral approach to foreign policy. For them America is still a "city on the hill," a model for the rest of the world, but also a place apart. And beneath the bellicosity of much Republican thinking on defense is a yearning for a safer, simpler world. The plan, first hatched by Reagan, to build a "missile shield" that will protect America from all possible enemies is the quintessential expression of this wish.

Republicans have always invoked the idea that measures of which they disapprove (such as Social Security, the League of Nations, and the minimum wage) violate American values. In a typically Republican rhetorical flourish, President Calvin Coolidge warned, "We do not need to import any foreign economic ideas or any foreign government. We had better stick to the American brand of government, the American brand of equality, and the American brand of wages. America had better stay American." Such unquestioning faith in the superiority of all things American has sometimes led Republicans to be suspicious of immigrants, especially when they come from very alien cultures. William McKinley declared his support for immigration laws that would "secure the United States from invasion by the debased and criminal classes of the world." It was Republicans who passed laws severely restricting immigration in the 1920s and who most strongly advocated the process of assimilation, or "Americanization."

If individualism, social order, and patriotism have been three of the distinctive strands that have animated the party since its inception, there has also been one never-ending point of ambivalence: How far should government interfere in the lives of Americans? Viewed in one

A family poses with their wagon at Loup Valley, Nebraska, in 1886. The Republican Party opposed the extension of slavery because it favored the unrestricted rights of free white Northerners to go west.

way, there is a straightforward answer to this question. Republicans have always disliked meddling government—it was, after all, Ronald Reagan who memorably declared that "government is not the solution, government is the problem." President Ulysses S. Grant declared in his second inaugural address in 1873 that "social equality is not a subject to be legislated upon," and eighty years later President Eisenhower made a similar point when he observed, "I don't believe you can change the hearts of men with laws or decisions."

Perhaps contradictorily, the Republicans have also been the party of prohibition and of laws restricting trade on Sundays. More recently, it has become the party that wants to impose a Christian form of worship in public schools, to ban abortion, and to use government to crack down on manifestations of what they regard as sexual immorality or social breakdown: divorce, pornography, and homosexuality. The truth is that while in the economic sphere Republicans have most certainly (with the notable exception of the great progressive president, Teddy Roosevelt) favored minimum government interference, this has often not been true when it comes to cultural and social issues.

These divisions can be traced back to the origins of the party as a coalition of old Democrats who hated slavery because they wanted people to be left alone and former Whigs who wanted to abolish it because they believed that the role of government was to create a better, more moral society. It is, then, from the traditions of Whiggish Yankee Protestantism that the party has derived its didactic tone and sense of mission—as well as its now sometimes forgotten role as the champion of public education. The nineteenth-century forebears of today's Republicans implored their fellow citizens to exercise the virtues of self-control, self-restraint, and self-mastery. The term "self-government," which peppered Republican speeches in the nineteenth century, had a double meaning. It referred to the individual as well as to the nation. The exemplar was Abraham Lincoln, who rose from a humble background through such astonishing feats of self-discipline as teaching himself the principles of the ancient Greek mathematician Euclid so that he might think in a more logical way.

Whenever the Republican Party has had electoral success, it has done so by mobilizing a broad cross-section of American society. In the 1984 election that swept Reagan to victory, he was supported by a majority in every socioeconomic group. In addition to the appeal of

Theodore Roosevelt made his name by forming a volunteer cavalry company in the Spanish-American War. In the White House, he built up American power and extended American influence abroad, establishing the pattern for later Republican presidents.

the warm concepts of individualism, social order, and patriotism—all values deeply ingrained in American culture—Republicans have fashioned a fourth, clinching argument: material well-being under their administration. Theodore Roosevelt cheerily brandished the "full dinner pail" that was the result of Republican economic policies like high tariffs. Other Republicans boasted of "a chicken in every pot" and later, "a car in every garage."

At their strongest when they have identified with the "little guy," Republicans have lost power when they have allowed their faith in the system to blind them to the reality of life for most Americans. The most notable example was in the long period between the 1930s and the 1960s, when Democrats offered practical programs that achieved what Republican laissez-faire economics had not—putting food on people's tables and providing them with work.

The New Deal was the great watershed in the history of the Republican Party—as in so many ways it was to the larger story of American political development. The New Deal profoundly and irrevocably altered the role of government in American life. Mainstream Republicans faced a hard truth in these long years in the wilderness: They could not win elections by telling people that government did not work, when, thanks to the New Deal, it was bringing practical benefits and hope to millions. Those in the Republican Party from the 1930s onward who have sought to roll back the state have therefore been, in the true sense of the word, radicals, for they have sought to dismantle the structures and habits that have become ingrained in American life. But the key to the Republican resurgence over the last four decades has been the party's ability to convince sufficient voters of comparatively modest means that Republicans were, once again, on their side, and that their best chance of success in what Lincoln called the "race of life" was with Republicans running the government.

The New Deal therefore transformed the Republican Party from the defenders of the status quo into radicals—at least in relation to the vitally important issue of the role of government in American life. It also led to the complete reversal of the parties' respective positions on the great American question of the balance of power between the federal government and the states. Until the New Deal, the Democrats were the party of localism, decentralization—even, if you believed some Republican propaganda, of secession. Republicans, who had led a war to restore the Union, were the great centralizers, the truly

President Nixon dines with Chinese prime minister Zhou Enlai during his memorable visit to China in 1972. Although he made his name as a "Red-baiter," Nixon later proved to be a master of pragmatic statesmanship.

national party. Since 1933 the size of the federal government has grown prodigiously, and in response Republicans have embraced the once-scorned notion of states' rights. Reagan called for a "new federalism" that would return power to the states. All Republicans now argue that decisions should ideally be made at the lowest possible level.

Today's Republican Party is obviously different in important ways from the party that was so dominant before the New Deal revolution. In the late nineteenth and early twentieth centuries, Republicans were strongest in New England and the Midwest, whereas the South and the big cities were Democratic territory. Since 1968 Republicans have gradually expanded their support in the South and Southwest so that they are now the dominant party across that vast and expanding region. At the same time, Democrats have increased their strength in the Northeast. In 1994, when the Republicans won back control of the House of Representatives for the first time in decades, the most remarkable feature of their victory was that they won a majority of House and Senate seats in both North and South, a feat they had not achieved since 1872. This change looks dramatic on a map—indeed, the parties have almost reversed themselves geographically—but underneath, there are still some continuities. Ethnic voters and new immigrants are reliably Democratic now, just as they were in the 1850s. Wealthy businessmen are reliably Republican now, just as they were then. The one section of the population that has deserted the Republican Party is African Americans, once loyal supporters of the party of Lincoln, now giving 90 percent of their votes to Democrats.

President George W. Bush and Senator Trent Lott of Mississippi celebrate the 100th birthday of the late senator Strom Thurmond of South Carolina. The South has become the new Republican heartland.

Republicans are strongest when they are honest about how America treats its weakest and most vulnerable citizens as well as how well it rewards its strongest. The progressive Republicans of the early twentieth century—epitomized by Theodore Roosevelt—realized that the freedom of the individual is at risk not just from an overmighty government but also from the power of Big Business and by the barriers to upward mobility placed by poverty. The party that began with Abraham Lincoln's promise to save the "last, best hope of Earth" has continued over 150 years to urge Americans to have faith in themselves, their free market system, and the moral example they believe they set for the world. No one in the modern era has captured that spirit more perfectly than Reagan, whose words—indeed whose entire presidency—glistened with optimism, faith in the future, and belief in the infallibility of the American way.

Chapter One

Lincoln and Liberty

1854–1865

Lincoln and Liberty
1854—1865

THE EXACT SPOT WHERE THE REPUBLICAN PARTY was founded is a matter of some dispute. Ripon, Wisconsin, and Jackson, Michigan, both claim to be the birthplace of the party. It was certainly in the Old Northwest, in the summer of 1854, that political organizations calling themselves "Republican" first emerged. There, in counties that had been settled predominantly by Protestant Yankees, antislavery feeling was running high in the wake of one of the most momentous pieces of congressional legislation in American history, the Kansas-Nebraska Act. This act gave slaveholders the right to take their human property into the newly organized Western territories of Kansas and Nebraska.

For Southerners who had long been urging the expansion of slavery, this was a sweet victory. For many Northerners it was an assault on the basic principles of the republic. It also struck the fatal blow to the old two-party system of Whigs and Democrats. Since the 1830s these national organizations had drawn support in roughly equal amounts from Dixie and the free states. Now both parties split on sectional lines, but the Whigs, weakened by defections, disappeared altogether. Many Northern Democrats also deserted their party in protest at what they saw as a craven concession to the slave interest. Together, dissident Democrats and Whigs looking for a new political home formed the earliest groups that adopted the label "Republican."

While some Republicans, such as Massachusetts senator Charles Sumner, were principally motivated by a moral objection to slavery, many more were antislavery because they believed that a society of entrepreneurs and small-scale capitalists could not thrive or even survive if slavery were allowed to spread and grow. Slavery violated the basic tenets of a free labor society—that labor was the source of value and that every man should have the right to earn his daily bread from the sweat of his own brow. The Constitution made it impossible for a party that was serious about power to propose abolishing slavery where it already existed, but Republicans stuck firm to the principle of opposing the expansion of slavery into any more Western territories. The name "Republican" symbolized the mission of the party.

The hut in Ripon, Wisconsin, where the very first meeting of the Republican Party is alleged to have taken place in 1854.

Previous pages: Fugitive slaves make their way to freedom across the Rappahannock River in Virginia early in the Civil War.

16

John C. Frémont became a national hero in the 1840s when he undertook a number of trailblazing expeditions in the West. Frémont reveled in the nickname "Pathfinder" and was fittingly the first to contest the presidency for the new Republican Party.

In the Kansas Territory in 1856, the conflict between free-soil and proslavery settlers descended into bloody civil war—an indication of what was to come.

Republicans saw themselves as redeeming the republic from the grip of the Southern slaveholders. Viewed in this light, Republicanism was nothing less than a moral crusade.

The party grew slowly in its first two years. Another new organization, the American, or "Know-Nothing," Party, appeared for a while to be the main challenger to the Democrats in the North. Know-Nothings, so called because they began as a secret fraternal society whose members were supposed to answer any probing questions by saying that they knew nothing, were a nativist organization that campaigned to restrict the rights of immigrants, many of them Irish Catholics, who were flooding into the ports of New York and Boston in these years. The Know-Nothings, though, also foundered and split on the rock of slavery expansion, with many joining the Republicans.

The first Republican candidate for president was the dashing explorer John C. Frémont, who ran in 1856. His campaign struck idealistic antislavery chords while also appealing to the material self-interest and anti-Catholic impulses of Northern workers. From their Whig forebears the Republicans inherited a commitment to the active use of government to foster economic development and individual opportunity. In 1856 they supported a plan to provide homesteads in the West to free white settlers and favored government support for a transcontinental railroad. The bright future of economic prosperity based on free labor was endangered, they warned ominously, by the encroachments of the proslavery conspirators.

Everywhere there were signs that North and South were on a fatal collision course. Opening up Kansas to slaves as well as free settlers had led to violent conflict between the two competing groups. In one particularly notorious incident, a family of proslavery settlers was massacred by John Brown, a zealous abolitionist who said he was obeying God's command. The proslavery forces exacted their revenge and the territory slid into civil war. Meanwhile, on the floor of the Senate chamber, Charles Sumner was attacked and beaten unconscious by Preston Brooks, a South Carolina congressman who had taken offense at a speech in which the great spokesman for black rights had condemned slaveowners as sinners. While Southerners presented Brooks with inscribed canes to replace the one he had broken on Sumner's head and congratulated him for defending Southern honor, the Republican Party rallied Northern voters by reminding them of "Bleeding Kansas" and "Bleeding Sumner."

Frémont's campaign helped to consolidate the new party, but a majority of Northerners remained unpersuaded by the Republican cause, frightened by the Democrats' dire warnings that the Union would break apart if an entirely sectional party were to win. The Democrats were the party of the Union in 1856; the Republicans, by whipping up opposition in the South and running candidates only in the North, were entrenching the sectional divide.

Over the next four years, the new party assiduously built up its support. It fused the populism of the old Jacksonian Democratic Party with the moral purpose of the Whigs, while Know-Nothings were courted with scurrilous anti-Catholic diatribes. If there was one event that helped this process of party-building and propelled the Republican Party into a majority position in the North, it was the Supreme Court's Dred Scott decision in 1857. In the most notorious and fateful judgment in the Court's history, Chief Justice Roger B. Taney, a Democrat, ruled that slave "property" was as inviolable as other types of property and that it was therefore unconstitutional for Congress to prohibit slavery in the territories. The implication was that slaveholders might legally be able to take their "property" into free states as well. By promising no less than the nationalization of slavery, the court went beyond what even most Southerners had previously demanded. It also declared constitutionally invalid the core of the new Republican Party's identity: opposition to the extension of slavery. Such an apparently crude exercise of Southern political power played into the hands of the new party. Here, surely, Republicans charged, was evidence of a conspiracy to destroy liberties of white Northerners.

It was at this critical moment that Abraham Lincoln strode onto the national stage. Born in a log cabin in Kentucky to illiterate parents, Lincoln's life story exemplified the virtues of self-discipline. With almost no formal schooling, the young Lincoln moved to Springfield, Illinois, married well, and rose to become a successful lawyer and a valued and respected member of the community. Lincoln's personal quest for self-improvement mirrored his conviction that the society around him could and should be continually improved, sentiments that made him a natural Whig in a Democratic state. His early political career in the Illinois legislature and in the U.S. Congress (where he spent only one term) was spent fighting for causes like a proper banking system. On the rights and wrongs of slavery, Lincoln said little. As with so many Northerners, the Kansas-Nebraska Act and

The earliest image we have of Abraham Lincoln, taken in 1846 when he was a successful lawyer and Illinois state legislator, with ambitions to rise even higher.

then the outrageous Dred Scott decision convinced him that the South's "peculiar institution" was strangling the lifeblood of the nation, and he did not flinch from condemning it as a moral wrong.

In a speech in Peoria, Illinois, in 1854, Lincoln expressed the shame and anger so many Northerners felt at the expansion of slavery. "Our Republican robe is soiled and trailed in the dust," he declared. "Let us repurify it. Let us turn and wash it white, in the spirit, if not the blood of the Revolution." Lincoln did not oppose slavery where it had always existed, in the Southern states, but he wanted it to be an exception to the general rule of freedom, on the path to eventual extinction. "Let us turn slavery from its claims of 'moral right,' back upon its existing legal rights, and its arguments of 'necessity.' Let us return it to the position our fathers gave it; and there let it rest in peace." He continued with words that, with their evocation of the universal mission of the American republic, foreshadowed his later wartime speeches and encapsulated the moral and nationalist purpose of what would shortly emerge as the Republican Party:

> Let us readopt the Declaration of Independence, and with it, the practices, and policy, which harmonize with it. Let North and South—let all Americans—let all lovers of liberty everywhere—join in the great and good work. If we do this, we shall not only have saved the Union; but we shall have so saved it as to make, and to keep it, forever worthy of the saving. We shall have so saved it, that the succeeding millions of free happy people, the world over, shall rise up, and call us blessed, to the latest generations.

Lincoln's genius for crafting speeches like this soon propelled him into the front rank of Illinois Republicans and made him the obvious man to challenge the sitting Democratic senator in 1858. That senator was none other than the author of the Kansas-Nebraska Act, Stephen A. Douglas. A series of debates between Lincoln and Douglas in front of large and enthusiastic crowds in towns all over Illinois dramatized the issues at stake in the wake of the Dred Scott decision. "A house divided against itself cannot stand," Lincoln proclaimed, in a prophetic warning that the North had to stand firm. Douglas was reelected, but the debates won Lincoln a national profile. Without them, he would not have won the Republican nomination in 1860, beating the favorite, Senator William Henry Seward of New York, who had led the party in

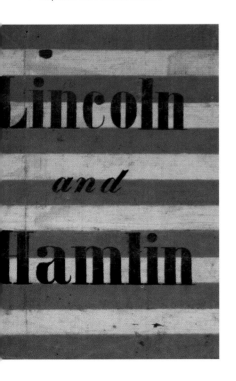

An 1860 presidential election campaign flag with thirty-one stars, representing the number of states in the Union that year, along with the names of the Republican candidates.

Congress with great sagacity, but who some delegates thought was too radical. Lincoln had no baggage; he was the perfect man to carry the crucial swing states in the election.

The election of 1860 was a political revolution. For the first time, a purely sectional party won enough votes in the electoral college to capture the White House. Against a divided Democratic Party, Lincoln captured more than half the popular votes and almost all the electoral college votes of the free states. He was not even on the ballot in the Deep South. Southerners were appalled. Convinced that the victory of the "black Republican Party" was an immediate threat to slavery, South Carolina and six other Deep South states seceded before Lincoln was even inaugurated. As the Democrats had predicted, the lawful election of a political party had broken the Union.

If the Republican Party was born in the political crisis sparked by the expansion of slavery, it was baptized in the fire of the Civil War. The four turbulent years of Lincoln's administration were the making of his party, giving it a store of memories for elections to come and bestowing on it the accolade of having saved the Union.

The war unexpectedly gave the new Republican Party an opportunity to pass a full legislative program almost unhindered by congressional opposition. The absence of Democratic congressmen from the seceding states left Republicans with large majorities, which they used to pass a raft of important economic programs, including the authorization to build the transcontinental railroad and the 1862 Homestead Act. Innovations that were to shape profoundly the future development of the nation had their origins in wartime. A federal income tax was introduced for the first time as a means of helping to finance the war. For similar reasons, Congress took the momentous step of authorizing a paper currency. The highly controversial "greenbacks" may have created inflation in the North, but they provided the unprecedented supply of credit required to enable Northern manufacturing capacity to meet the challenges of supplying an army of more than a million men.

Lincoln had to steer a difficult course in the first year of war. On one side the radical faction of his party pushed for emancipation to become a stated war aim, while on the other side conservatives urged restraint. Initially, Lincoln, conscious of the need to keep the North united behind the war effort, endorsed the notion of a limited war; but by the summer of 1862, when it was increasingly clear that there would

"YOUR PLAN"

A cartoon lambasting Lincoln's Democratic opponent in 1864, General George B. McClellan, for cozying up to Confederates over the issue of black rights. Lincoln, by contrast, gives the rebels a pointedly short shrift.

A banner supporting Lincoln's reelection in 1864. The farmer with his plow in the bottom panel holds out the promise of peace and prosperity once the Union is restored.

MINE.

be no easy military victory for the Union, the president became convinced that he would have to use the ultimate weapon of slave emancipation against the rebels.

The Emancipation Proclamation, issued on January 1, 1863, transformed the war and divided the North. Applying only to slaves in rebel territory and not to slaves in states, or occupied parts of states, that remained in the Union, the proclamation was issued by the president under his interpretation of the "war powers" granted to him by the Constitution. He justified it on grounds of "military necessity." Radicals and abolitionists within the Republican Party were jubilant. At a meeting in Boston on New Year's Eve, 1862, veteran abolitionist William Lloyd Garrison wept tears of joy as the proclamation came into force on the stroke of midnight. Lincoln, though, was very aware that many Northerners did not want to fight to free the slaves. Campaigning in the fall elections of 1862, Democrats predicted that emancipation would lead to an "invasion" of the North by freed slaves competing for jobs and degrading Northern labor.

Ever the pragmatist, President Lincoln judiciously let it be known that he favored plans to colonize freed slaves outside the borders of the United States. He told a group of blacks in August 1862 that the "broad physical difference" between the two races was a "great disadvantage to us both, as I think, your race suffer very greatly, many of them, by living among us, while ours suffers from your presence." In practice, colonization schemes never came to much; while Lincoln, in the face of enormous pressure, never once wavered in his commitment to emancipation and was not afraid to bluntly point out the contribution that black people were making to the war, especially after the enrollment of black Union troops in the spring of 1863.

By 1864, as slavery collapsed behind Confederate lines and black troops valiantly fought under the Union flag, Democratic opposition to emancipation became more and more desperate and more openly racist. Democratic cartoonists in the election campaign of 1864 depicted rapacious black men seducing white women. That the women in question almost always seemed to be willing partners suggests the depths of the sexual anxiety they were probing. Meanwhile, Republican cartoonists drew black soldiers standing proudly to attention while Lincoln bayoneted a bedraggled and submissive rebel.

The extraordinary spectacle of a presidential election taking place in the midst of a war was a tribute to the resilience of the American political system. No one ever suggested abandoning elections in wartime. After all, the war was being fought, Lincoln had declared, to ensure that "ballots are the peaceful and rightful successors of bullets." That did not mean, however, that partisanship was also acceptable in wartime, and in fact Northerners were united only by the firm conviction that party organization was a danger to the war effort. A widely read pamphlet that summed up the prevailing attitude toward party politics in wartime was entitled "No Party Now But All For Our Country." Responding to this popular mood, Republicans abandoned their name for the duration of the war and adopted the title "Union Party." The reelection of Lincoln in wartime was not a party question, Republicans insisted, but rather one of patriotism.

The other side of this strategy of wrapping themselves in the nation's flag was discrediting the Democrats as disloyal. In some respects such an attack was unfair; most Democrats did in fact support the Union but were opposed to the radicalism of the administration, particularly the policy of emancipation. The fact remained, though, that the last, best hope the Confederates had of winning the war was the election of Democrats in the North.

In 1864 the Democratic candidate was George B. McClellan, who as a Union general had aroused the ire of Lincoln for his extreme reluctance to engage the enemy in battle. McClellan said he supported the restoration of the Union, but his platform committed him to "an immediate cessation of hostilities." Given McClellan's stance, had Lincoln lost in November 1864, it is unlikely that the war would have ended in a decisive victory for the Union. Not surprisingly, in the circumstances, this was a fiercely fought election. McClellan was even referred to as the "leader of the Confederate forces." This kind of hyperbole was stoked by reports that treasonous organizations in the Midwest were fomenting rebellion and by genuine anxieties in both parties about the other resorting to arms.

In the end, Lincoln won with a comfortable but not overwhelming margin of 55 percent of the popular vote. More than 70 percent of the Union army voted for "Uncle Abe," as they came to call this folksy but clear-sighted leader. To supporters of Lincoln, party political conflict in wartime was a desperate struggle between patriots and traitors, and the Democrats were a dangerous internal threat. After Lincoln's reelection, Charles Sumner hailed the death of the Democratic Party as "now buried where it cannot be reached again. Loathsome and putrid from corruption, it had been a nuisance while it was above ground. . . . The Democratic Party had ceased to be loyal.

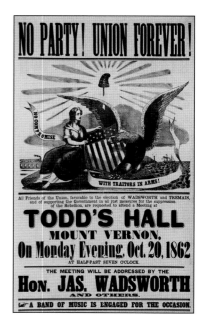

"No Party! Union Forever!" The slogan advertising this political meeting in 1862 reveals a widespread popular distrust of party politics in wartime.

John Wilkes Booth, Lincoln's assassin, saw his desperate act as a way of redeeming Southern honor and pride—by killing the man who had destroyed his beloved Confederacy.

The box at Ford's Theatre where Lincoln was shot on Good Friday, 1865. The framed portrait of George Washington on the balcony was there at the time.

It was no longer patriotic. . . . It should no longer exist." In contrast, Lincoln's powerful language weaved a new vision of American nationality, one based on the promise that all men are created equal. In 1860 Republicans had been castigated by their opponents for threatening to destroy the nation. By 1865 they had imposed their conception of American identity on the nation as a whole.

On the night of April 14, 1865, Good Friday, the president and Mrs. Lincoln went out to watch a British comedy, *Our American Cousin*, starring Laura Keene, at Ford's Theatre in Washington. In the middle of the performance, John Wilkes Booth, a well-known actor whose performances in Shakespearean tragedies the president had enjoyed, slipped unnoticed into the back of the presidential box and shot the president in the back of the head before leaping to the stage. One of his spurs caught on the curtains and he fell heavily to the stage, breaking an ankle. With a cry of *"Sic semper tyrannis,"* Booth hobbled from the stage and made his escape by horseback. In a simultaneous attack, the secretary of state, William Seward, narrowly escaped death.

The mortally wounded president was carried to a house across the road from the theater, where he died shortly before 7:30 the following morning. In the quiet of the small room, the secretary of war, Edwin M. Stanton, pronounced his epitaph: "Now he belongs to the ages." The tolling of church bells spread the news across the city and, soon, the nation. An aura of emotion surrounded the dead president's final protracted journey back to Springfield, Illinois.

Booth was the self-appointed avenging angel of the defeated South. His fanatical pro-Confederate zeal was combined with an unstable personality and a weakness for overacting. After two weeks on the run he was tracked by federal troops to a tobacco barn in Virginia, and when the barn was set afire, he was shot trying to flee. Hours later Booth was dead. Four coconspirators (including a woman, Mary Surratt) were hanged after a military tribunal. A badly organized plot had achieved a dastardly end. The peace that Lincoln found on Good Friday threw into doubt the meaning of the peace that was just at that moment descending on four years of war.

The name of Abraham Lincoln is forever more enshrined in the nation's memory as the wise and humane leader who not only saved the Union but created a better, redeemed republic in its place. He was the first and the greatest of Republicans.

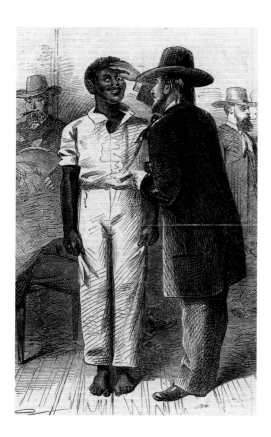

Slaves for Sale

A slave dealer inspects his goods before making a purchase at a slave market in Virginia (above). This drawing and hundreds of others like it, appearing in popular illustrated weekly magazines like *Harper's Weekly*, disturbed many Northerners. The new Republican Party did not seek to abolish slavery outright, but most of its supporters did see it as a morally unjust institution that must be prevented from expanding. This kind of image, which demonstrated that slaves were mere chattels, outraged Northerners who believed that every man had a right to the fruits of his own labor.

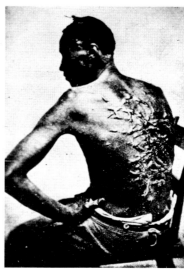

The South's "Peculiar Institution"

A gang of slaves picking cotton (left), the crop that made the use of black slaves so profitable for Southern planters. This image appears peaceful enough, and postwar nostalgia for the Old South—given wide currency through such films as *Gone with the Wind*—dwelled on it. The overseer riding past provides a hint of menace, however, and the scars on this slave's back (above) demonstrate that the institution was based on naked violence.

The Face of Abolitionism

Harriet Beecher Stowe (right) was described by Abraham Lincoln as the "little woman who made this big war." Her novel *Uncle Tom's Cabin*, first serialized and then published in 1852, had a huge impact on public opinion in the North. The book sold 300,000 copies in the first year alone and was quickly adapted as a play, a musical, and as a "magic lantern" slide show. The poster (above) is for a theater production in the late 1850s. The very white-looking face of the heroine and the chocolate-box sentimentality of the drawing suggest that slavery was offensive to many Northerners because it violated Victorian ideas of family, domesticity, and female virtue.

The Face of Slavery

Dred Scott (above) was a slave who sued for his freedom on the grounds that his master had taken him into a free territory. In a notorious decision, the Supreme Court decided in 1857 that this did not entitle Scott to freedom and that a black man had "no rights which the white man was bound to respect." These orphan children (left), brother and sister, were liberated by Union troops in 1864. They were handed over to the Society of Friends to be educated at the Orphan's Shelter in Philadelphia. This photograph was widely sold as a postcard to raise money for the orphanage.

The Pathfinder

The Republican candidate in the 1856 election was the Western explorer John C. Frémont, seen here on a party banner with his running mate, William Dayton. Already a well-known public figure as a result of his exploration of the Oregon Territory, Frémont had a name that lent itself to the message of the new party. In the 1856 election the Republicans adopted the slogan "Free Soil, Free Labor, Free Men, Frémont."

The Know-Nothings

Fighting Republicans for the votes of Northerners in the election of 1856 was the American Party (left, an illustration of a mass meeting of the party in New York). The powerful spotlight was intended to symbolize the light of truth shining on the party, which favored restricting the political rights of immigrants. The American Party was more commonly known as the "Know-Nothings" because members were supposed to deny knowing anything of party politics. Know-Nothingism was a rejection of traditional partisan politics. The anti-immigrant song "Citizen Know Nothing" (sheet music cover, above) indicates a defiant pride in the party's nickname.

The North Divides Over Slavery

This 1856 Republican cartoon (right) shows leading Northern Democratic politicians, including Stephen A. Douglas and President James Buchanan, forcing slavery down the throat of a Kansas "Free-Soiler"—a settler from the Northern states who wanted the new territory to be off-limits to slavery. The cartoon shows some sympathy for the slave, but is drawing more attention to the plight of the bound and gagged Free-Soiler. The message is clear: Democrats are preventing ordinary Northerners from exercising their right to move west.

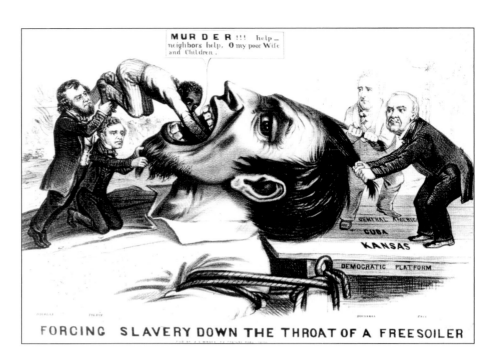

FORCING SLAVERY DOWN THE THROAT OF A FREESOILER

John Brown Stokes the Fires

Abolitionist John Brown (opposite) believed that he was God's agent on earth. He dedicated his life to the destruction of slavery. In 1859 Brown led a badly organized raid, secretly supported by some Republican radicals, on a federal arsenal at Harper's Ferry in Virginia, intending to use the weapons to arm slaves and lead an uprising. He was quickly captured by federal troops led by Colonel Robert E. Lee, tried, and sentenced to death. The painting (right) by Thomas Hovenden shows Brown bestowing his blessing on a black baby as he is led to his fate. Images like this show Brown as he wanted to be remembered, as a martyr to the cause of freedom. When church bells rang out across the North to mark his death, many in the South became more convinced than ever that they had no future in the Union and that the Republican Party was bent on destroying their way of life in its entirety.

PROGRESSIVE DEMOCRACY—PROSPECT OF A SMASH UP.

The Election of 1860

This cartoon (above) shows the Democratic platform about to be blasted in two by the approaching Republican train. The failure of the Democratic Party to agree on a single candidate in the 1860 election helped Lincoln's cause. The Republican message was promoted by marching companies known as "Wide Awakes" (left), seen here parading in New York City. They wore capes to protect them from the kerosene dripping from their torches. Lincoln's main opponent was Stephen A. Douglas, with whom he had memorably debated the slavery issue in Illinois two years before. Disaffected Southern Democrats quit the national convention and nominated Vice President Breckinridge on a proslavery ticket. To complete the quartet, the remnants of the Whig Party nominated John Bell of Tennessee to represent the Constitutional Union Party, which sought compromise between points of view that were threatening to tear the nation apart.

Abraham Lincoln

Stephen A. Douglas

John C. Breckinridge

John Bell

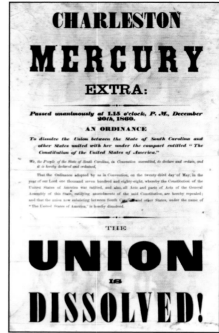

Twin Inaugurations

An extra edition of the *Charleston Mercury* announces the momentous news that the state has seceded (top right). South Carolina was the first to secede but it was quickly followed by other Deep South states. On February 18, 1861, Jefferson Davis (above right) was inaugurated as the first and only president of the Confederate States of America in Montgomery, Alabama (above). Davis was a Mississippi planter with a long career in the army and federal politics behind him, but nothing had prepared him for the stress of leading the Confederacy through a traumatic war. Three weeks later in Washington, Abraham Lincoln was inaugurated on the steps of the Capitol (right), with its unfinished dome a fitting symbol for the perilously fragmented Union.

The First Shot

The Civil War started when Confederates fired on Fort Sumter in Charleston Harbor. This bastion of federal power in the South fell on April 14, 1861, and a Confederate flag now waved above the surrendered fort (left). Three years later, in 1864, Union cannons on nearby Morris Island open up on Fort Sumter (below), which was well fortified against attackers (right) and remained in Confederate hands until the war's end.

First Blood in the North

This engraving is, with grim irony, titled "The Lexington of 1861," referring to the first battle of the American Revolution. In this case, the first "battle" of the Civil War being referred to is not between Confederate and Union troops but between the Sixth Massachusetts Volunteer Infantry Regiment and angry pro-Southern rioters in Baltimore, Maryland, in April 1861. Pro-secession feeling in Maryland was gradually repressed during the war, but as this engraving reveals, it came as an unwelcome shock to prowar Northerners to find that they could not even rely on the support of their neighbors in the border states in their effort to suppress the rebellion.

PUBLISHED BY CURRIER & IVES,

THE LE

The Massachusetts Volunteers fighting their way through the Street

152 NASSAU ST NEW YORK.

INGTON OF 1861.

Baltimore, on their march to the defence of the National Capitol April 19.th 1861. Hurrah for the Glorious 6.th

The Union at War

After the battle of Antietam in September 1862, President Lincoln confers with General George B. McClellan (left, facing Lincoln). The general, who delighted in the nickname "Little Napoleon," was, in fact, so reluctant to engage with enemy troops that Lincoln, in despair, eventually had to fire him. Lincoln finally discovered in Ulysses S. Grant a general who was prepared to fight hard enough to beat the Confederates into submission. Grant (below left, at his headquarters with the Army of the Potomac in 1864), was nicknamed "Unconditional Surrender Grant" in acknowledgment of his implacable will to prevail over the enemy. Life at the front was not without its distractions from war. Officers of the Army of the Potomac, somewhere behind the lines during the siege of Petersburg in 1864, place bets on a cockfight (right).

The Emancipation Proclamation

Frank Carpenter's 1863 painting of Lincoln with his cabinet, about to sign the Emancipation Proclamation, which declared "thenceforward, and forever free" all slaves in Confederate territory. Clockwise from left: Secretary of War Edwin M. Stanton, Secretary of the Treasury Salmon P. Chase, Lincoln, Secretary of the Navy Gideon Welles, Secretary of the Interior Caleb B. Smith, Postmaster General Montgomery Blair, Attorney General Edward Bates, Secretary of State William H. Seward.

Blacks in the Civil War

In the aftermath of the Emancipation Proclamation, which came into effect on January 1, 1863, Lincoln authorized the enlistment of black troops in segregated units with white officers, and, initially, a lower rate of pay than their white comrades. The 107th U.S. Colored Infantry poses proudly (above). Frederick Douglass (left), an escaped slave and vocal abolitionist, took a lead role in recruiting black troops. He had several meetings with Lincoln and later recalled that he was "the first great man that I talked with in the United States freely, who in no single instance reminded me of the difference between himself and myself, of the difference of color."

United in Death

Confederate and Union dead share the trenches outside Petersburg, Virginia, in early 1865. Photographs like this brought home the reality of war to the Northern public. Matthew Brady was a leading war photographer. He exhibited his work, and that of his assistants, at his galleries in Washington and New York. The first exhibition was of the aftermath of the Battle of Antietam, fought in September 1862. *The New York Times* reported that "Mr. Brady has done something to bring home to us the terrible reality and earnestness of war. If he has not brought bodies and laid them in our dooryard and along the streets he has done something very like it."

A Troubled Home Front

The North remained deeply divided by the Lincoln administration's war policy. In July 1863 draft riots in New York City (left) had to be put down by Union troops returning from Gettysburg. Meanwhile the administration, desperate to find new ways of financing the war, was driven to introducing controversial innovations like a graduated income tax and "greenbacks," or U.S. Treasury–backed paper money. The first dollar bills (center left) bore the image of Salmon P. Chase, secretary of the treasury. In the face of horrific battlefield carnage, volunteer organizations such as the U.S. Christian Commission (bottom left) and the U.S. Sanitary Commission (right, accompanying Grant's army in the Wilderness Campaign in 1864) did invaluable work in caring for casualties.

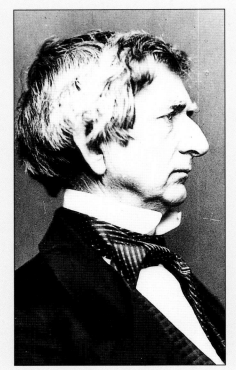

William H. Seward

Charles Sumner

Salmon P. Chase

Edwin M. Stanton

Wartime Leaders

In this 1863 photograph (right) by Alexander Gardner, the strain of war shows in President Lincoln's lined face and haunted eyes. He had been deeply affected by the death in 1862 of his beloved son Willie, who succumbed to the typhoid fever that was rampant in swampy Washington, D.C. William H. Seward (top left) was Lincoln's able secretary of state. One of the leading Republicans in the Senate before the war, he had been the favorite for the Republican nomination in 1860 and was bitterly disappointed when he lost out to Lincoln. Nevertheless, Seward became Lincoln's closest cabinet ally during the war. Edwin M. Stanton (bottom right) was appointed secretary of war in December 1861. As a former Democrat, he symbolized the attempt of the Republican Party to broaden its appeal. He was ferociously efficient at his job and a leading supporter of emancipation and black rights. Salmon P. Chase (bottom left), secretary of the treasury, was a deeply religious man driven by ambition. He attempted to displace Lincoln as the Republican nominee in 1864 and accordingly stepped down from the cabinet. In a magnanimous gesture, Lincoln later appointed him chief justice of the Supreme Court. Charles Sumner (top right), a Republican senator from Massachusetts, regarded himself as the radical conscience of his party. He often criticized Lincoln for not moving more quickly to end slavery.

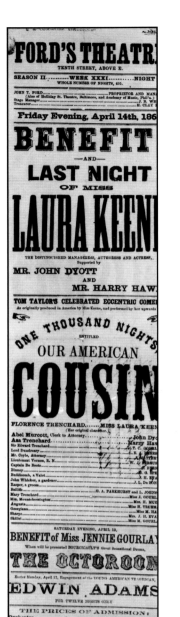

SURRAT.   BOOTH.   HAROLD.

War Department, Washington, April 20, 1865,

👉 $100,000 REWARD!

THE MURDERER

Of our late beloved President, Abraham Lincoln,

IS STILL AT LARGE.

$50,000 REWARD

Will be paid by this Department for his apprehension, in addition to any reward offered by Municipal Authorities or State Executives.

$25,000 REWARD

Will be paid for the apprehension of JOHN H. SURRATT, one of Booth's Accomplices.

$25,000 REWARD

Will be paid for the apprehension of David C. Harold, another of Booth's accomplices.

LIBERAL REWARDS will be paid for any information that shall conduce to the arrest of either of the above-named criminals, or their accomplices.

All persons harboring or secreting the said persons, or either of them, or aiding or assisting their concealment or escape, will be treated as accomplices in the murder of the President and the attempted assassination of the Secretary of State, and shall be subject to trial before a Military Commission and the punishment of DEATH.

Let the stain of innocent blood be removed from the land by the arrest and punishment of the murderers.

All good citizens are exhorted to aid public justice on this occasion. Every man should consider his own conscience charged with this solemn duty, and rest neither night nor day until it be accomplished.

EDWIN M. STANTON, Secretary of War.

DESCRIPTIONS.—BOOTH is Five Feet 7 or 8 inches high, slender build, high forehead, black hair, black eyes, and wears a heavy black moustache.

JOHN H. SURRAT is about 5 feet, 9 inches. Hair rather thin and dark; eyes rather light; no beard. Would weigh 145 or 150 pounds. Complexion rather pale and clear, with color in his cheeks. Wore light clothes of fine quality. Shoulders square; cheek bones rather prominent; chin narrow; ears projecting at the top; forehead rather low and square, but broad. Parts his hair on the right side; neck rather long. His lips are firmly set. A slim man.

DAVID C. HAROLD is five feet six inches high, hair dark, eyes dark, eyebrows rather heavy, full face, nose short, hand short and fleshy, feet small, instep high, round bodied, naturally quick and active, slightly closes his eyes when looking at a person.

NOTICE.—In addition to the above, State and other authorities have offered rewards amounting to almost one hundred thousand dollars, making an aggregate of about **TWO HUNDRED THOUSAND DOLLARS.**

Death of a President

Abraham Lincoln's murder on Good Friday, 1865, was a shattering blow to Northerners who had been celebrating the final collapse of the Confederacy. The president and Mrs. Lincoln had been attending a performance of *Our American Cousin*, starring the famous English actress Laura Keene (opposite, left) at Ford's Theatre in Washington (opposite, top right). His assassin, John Wilkes Booth, escaped and fled, but it quickly became clear that he had not acted alone. A small band of conspirators had also plotted to kill William H. Seward and General Grant. Booth was shot and killed by federal troops. Four of his coconspirators were hanged (opposite, bottom). A huge reward (left) formed part of the massive effort to track down the gang.

A Nation Mourns

A drawing by Thomas Nast, published in *Harper's Weekly*, shows the goddess Liberty weeping at the coffin of the slain president (above). Lincoln's open casket lying in state (right) at City Hall in New York on April 24, 1865, en route from Washington to his home in Springfield, Illinois. The funeral procession makes its way into Union Square in New York (opposite). In an upstairs window the future Republican president, six-year-old Teddy Roosevelt, looked down at this scene and was to remember it for the rest of his life.

Chapter Two

Robber Barons and Radicals

1865–1893

Robber Barons and Radicals
1865—1893

THE CIVIL WAR LEFT BEHIND a transformed American landscape. Southern will was utterly broken. When Confederate President Jefferson Davis issued a final desperate plea to his people to continue a guerrilla campaign against the Yankee invaders, none of his generals obeyed him. Thanking them for their "constancy and devotion" to their country, General Robert E. Lee bid his soldiers farewell and told them to go peacefully home, and the Confederate army dispersed over countryside that was devastated by war. One quarter of all Southern white men of military age had been killed. Countless more were wounded. Almost all had lost most of their wealth and much of their pride and confidence in the future.

Slavery and secession were the unequivocal twin casualties of the war. At the insistence of Southern slaveholders, slavery had been protected in the Constitution of 1787. Although the words "slave" and "slavery" were nowhere mentioned in it, several clauses—including a requirement that states return fugitives to the masters to whom they owed labor—entrenched the institution in the constitutional fabric of the young United States. Now, in 1865, the tangled compromise with slave labor that Republicans believed had tainted the American republic was utterly extinguished. The Thirteenth Amendment to the Constitution, which abolished slavery, was passed by Congress in January 1865. Slavery lingered on in a few scattered places until the amendment was ratified by the requisite number of states in December 1865, but for the vast majority of the four million slaves in the South, the day of jubilee came sooner. Everywhere in the South people were moving. Former slaves left their plantations to search for separated relatives, for paid work, or simply to experience their newfound freedom in a tangible way.

At the same time, the total military defeat of the Confederacy ensured that never again could secession be a political possibility, while victory brought a surge of nationalism among Northerners who had a novel sense of the power and permanence of their government. Before the war, the federal government had been a weak, remote entity; the only connection most citizens were likely to have had with it

Previous pages: The board of the Union Pacific Railroad meets in a private railroad car in 1868. Second from left is Thomas Durant, who was later involved in the Credit Mobilier scandal.

"Worse than slavery": Thomas Nast, the man who invented the modern political cartoon, penned this startling depiction of white Southern resistance to Reconstruction. A grinning Ku Klux Klansman and a member of the paramilitary White League join hands over a terrorized black family.

was when their mail was delivered by the U.S. Post Office. There were no federal taxes because the federal government did not need the money. By 1865 the relationship between the government and the people had changed forever. More than a million Northerners had fought for the United States. More than 300,000 of them had died. Those who were left had a new sense of the power of their national government and were endowed with a new commitment to its permanence. The wartime generation had seen their country with their own eyes. Farm boys from Wisconsin who had never traveled more than a few dozen miles from home in their lives had tramped and ridden over thousands of miles. This new Northern sense of nationalism flowered in the postwar years. Before the Civil War, the United States was usually referred to in the plural: "the United States are . . ."; after the war it became singular: "the United States is . . ."

Northern victory brought about the death of slavery and secession but it left other, crucial issues unresolved. What should be the status of black people in the emancipated South? What, in other words, did emancipation actually mean in practice? It was also unclear how and on what terms the defeated Confederate states should be allowed to resume their former status within the Union. These were the big questions that confronted the Republican Party and consumed the postwar generation in the South during Reconstruction.

In his second inaugural address a month before he was killed, President Lincoln had spoken words that many were later to interpret as the outline of what would have been a generous Reconstruction policy: "with malice toward none, with charity for all." We cannot, of course, ever know how he would have handled the issues of Reconstruction had he lived, but there is reason to believe that when Lincoln spoke of a "just and lasting peace" he meant justice for the former slaves as well as for white Southerners. In one of his final letters, Lincoln privately suggested to the Unionist governor of Louisiana that he might consider enfranchising at least those freedmen who had fought in the Union army. In doing so, Lincoln tentatively endorsed the policy of many radical Republicans.

If Southerners, black and white, thought that Confederate defeat would mark a return to something like normality, they were very wrong. In the coming years white Southerners were to feel that their world had been turned upside down. The new Republican Party was to become the agent of revolution.

Lincoln's death came at a moment when the party system seemed in flux. No less a figure than William H. Seward, the secretary of state, believed that the end of slavery had removed the need for the party he had helped to found in the 1850s. Instead, Seward and his political friends wanted the Union Party (the banner under which Lincoln and the Democrat Andrew Johnson had fought the 1864 presidential campaign) to become a new national organization that would, like the old Whig Party, draw support from both North and South. The new party would be conservative on the dangerous issues of the status of black people after slavery but, like the Whig Party, keen on fostering economic prosperity. The radicals in the Republican Party had decidedly different ideas. Far from disappearing in the wake of its great triumph, the Republican Party was reborn during the years of Reconstruction, its mission revived by, ironically, a bitter conflict between the majority of Republicans in Congress and the man who succeeded Lincoln in the White House.

Few men have risen further to become president of the United States than Andrew Johnson. Born into grinding poverty in North Carolina, he moved to Tennessee as a young man and was apprenticed as a tailor before climbing the rungs of the political ladder as a Democrat, an enthusiastic supporter of President Andrew Jackson. Johnson was a strong advocate of the rights of poor white farmers and an irrepressible foe of the slave-owning aristocrats who wielded, he felt, undue political influence in the South. Johnson disliked slavery only because it elevated class divisions among whites. Slavery's greatest crime, he believed, was attempting to destroy the Union. The only congressman to remain in Washington after his state seceded, Johnson was appointed military governor of Tennessee by President Lincoln after its occupation by Union troops. In the election of 1864 this redoubtable Southern Unionist was judged by Republican Party leaders to be the ideal man to be Lincoln's running mate. As a Southerner, a Unionist, and a Democrat, he symbolized the transformation of the sectional Republican Party into the Union Party.

When the new president assumed office, Congress was not in session and would not be for another eight months. In the intervening time Johnson demonstrated his obvious sympathy for defeated white Southerners and his complete lack of interest in the fate of freedmen, most dramatically by reversing General William T. Sherman's General Order No. 15, which had settled more than 10,000 black families on

Carpetbaggers—Northerners who came to the South to seek their fortune after the Civil War—have never had good press. This cartoon from 1865 uses the carpetbagger stereotype to attack radical Republican politician Carl Schurz, who moved from Wisconsin to Missouri after the war.

land abandoned by rebel planters. Defeated Confederates grew confident in the face of the president's leniency. Georgia even tried to return the Confederate vice president, Alexander H. Stephens, to the U.S. Senate. The Senate and the House both refused to seat any congressmen from the former Confederate states.

When Congress finally convened in December 1865, the leaders of the Republican majority soon began to wrest control of the Reconstruction process from the White House. For Johnson, the problem of Reconstruction was simply a matter of returning the Confederate states to their former status as soon as possible. For most Republicans on Capitol Hill, the issue was how the fruits of victory could be best secured. To this end they divided the former Confederate states into military districts, presided over by an army officer who supervised elections in which freedmen were allowed to vote. Congress also extended the life of the Freedmen's Bureau, a federal agency first established during the war to take care of the hundreds of thousands of black refugees. The bureau tried to protect the rights of the freedmen, supervising the drawing up of new labor contracts, arbitrating in disputes between blacks and whites, and even establishing freedmen's schools.

All this President Johnson vetoed. In the midterm elections of 1866, he took to the campaign trail attacking Republicans in highly personal terms. Only two years before, Johnson and his congressional opponents had stood together in the Union Party. Now there was an irreparable breach. While Johnson and a few allies, including Seward, still clung to the Union Party label and tried to make alliances with moderate Southerners, most began calling themselves Republicans again and returned to the party's old sectional rhetoric.

Boosted by a resounding victory in the 1866 congressional elections, Republicans pressed ahead with their Reconstruction policy and overrode the president's vetoes. In 1868 growing frustration with the president's obstructionism eventually led Republicans in the House of Representatives to impeach him on rather spurious grounds. Johnson was not a criminal; the only "crime" he was alleged to have committed was sacking his secretary of war (the radical Edwin Stanton) without the agreement of Congress in contravention of a dubiously constitutional law that had been passed to prevent him from doing just that. He certainly had not committed the "high crimes and misdemeanors" that the Constitution lays down as the only grounds on which a president, duly elected by the people, can be removed from

The Senate meets as a court of impeachment for the trial of President Andrew Johnson in 1868. He escaped being removed from office by just one vote.

office. Republicans were playing a potentially dangerous game in using impeachment as a political weapon. Had they succeeded, they would have established a precedent that may have led to a completely different relationship between the president and Congress. Like a prime minister in a parliamentary system, the president might have stayed in office only so long as he commanded the support of the legislature. This intriguing political possibility was avoided because Johnson was acquitted in the Senate by the tantalizingly close margin of one vote. He was left in office, but his power was weakened.

During Reconstruction the Republican Party was organized and gained power across the South. This was possible only because former slaves were granted the vote. African Americans made up 80 percent of the Republican voters in the South. Some were also elected to important offices, including the U.S. Senate. Most of these new black officeholders came from the small community of free blacks during the days of slavery. Often they had been ministers of religion or were skilled artisans such as cobblers or carpenters. Some, though, were former slaves. To most white Southerners, black men becoming lieutenant governors and congressmen was an outrage too horrendous to be tolerated. No matter that most Southern Republican leaders during Reconstruction were white, a myth of "black supremacy" developed, and for decades afterward this great experiment in political equality was castigated as a "tragic era." Films like *The Birth of a Nation* later entrenched this utterly unfounded version of history in the popular consciousness. That it survived so long is an extraordinary testimony to the enduring racism of American society. The other villains in this mythical history were "carpetbaggers" (Northerners who had descended upon the South after the war, often to make money from cotton), and "scalawags" (Southerners who supported the Republican Party). Most carpetbaggers did come to make money, but many others were long-standing abolitionists who came to work with and help the freedmen, frequently as schoolteachers. Scalawags were often from the upcountry areas where Unionist sympathy had remained strong during the war. Others simply saw the Republican Party as the agency of economic regeneration in the South.

Republican control of Southern state governments lasted only a few years. By the mid-1870s all but three Southern states had been redeemed by the Democrats. With the help of militia organizations like the Ku Klux Klan, Democrats used violence and intimidation to

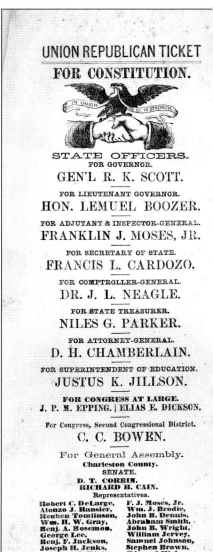

A South Carolina Union Republican ticket for the midterm elections of 1870. Southern whites bitterly resented the presence of black legislators in the Republican ranks.

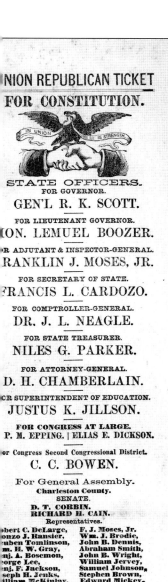

unite white voters and deter blacks from going to the polls. Meanwhile, the war hero General Ulysses S. Grant was elected president as a Republican in 1868 and reelected in 1872. Grant's administrations were riddled with corruption scandals, but the president remained determined to uphold the newly granted rights of blacks in the South. He used federal troops to try to break up the Klan in South Carolina, and in 1874 he sent them into Louisiana to uphold the Republican government there against an armed Democratic opposition.

By this time, though, the Northern wing of the Republican Party was fracturing and support for Reconstruction was seeping away fast. Grant faced a challenge in the 1872 election from a breakaway Liberal Republican Party that campaigned against political corruption and argued that Reconstruction had gone too far. After the economic slump of 1873, the plight of blacks in the South became of less pressing concern to Northern Republicans than the social implications of the dramatic industrialization that was transforming the nation. At the same time a number of well-publicized examples of corruption among Republican governments in the South played to ingrained racist prejudices about the inherent untrustworthiness of blacks.

In 1876 a closely fought presidential election resulted in deadlock, with both parties claiming the electoral votes of Louisiana, Florida, and South Carolina—the three Southern states still in Republican hands. After several months of political intrigue, a congressional committee decided the matter in favor of Rutherford B. Hayes, the Republican candidate (who was immediately dubbed "Rutherfraud B. Hayes" by bitter Democrats). A bargain had been struck. In return for conceding the election, Democrats were promised that the Northern effort to enforce black rights would come to an end. In 1877 the last federal troops were withdrawn from the South. Black Southerners lost the vote and a system of legalized discrimination known as Jim Crow established white domination in the South for generations. With few black voters left, the Republican Party collapsed in the South, which for the next century remained solidly loyal to the Democrats—the party that had redeemed the white race from the horror of having to share political power with blacks.

For Northern Republicans, Reconstruction had really been about re-creating the South in the Northern image. They wanted to establish a free labor system in the wake of the destruction of slavery and to prevent a resurgence of secessionist sentiment by destroying the political power of the old slave-owning class. Congressman Thaddeus

Stevens, the wily old radical from Pennsylvania who had been campaigning for the political rights of blacks since long before the war, was in the vanguard of those who urged Congress to sweep away the feudalism of the Old South. "The whole fabric of Southern society must be changed, and never can it be done if this opportunity is lost," he warned in a trenchant speech. "How can Republican institutions, free schools, free churches, free social intercourse exist in a mingled community of nabobs and serfs? If the South is ever to be made a safe republic, let her lands be cultivated by the toil of her owners or the free labor of intelligent citizens. This must be done even though it drive her nobility into exile."

Most Republicans had come into politics sharing the assumptions that underlay Stevens's argument. For them a republic could only survive if it consisted of equal, free, and independent citizens. Free labor was superior to either slave labor or a society of wage-earning proletarians, not only because it led to economic prosperity but also because it ensured that each citizen would have the economic independence to stand up for himself politically. Republicans had grown up in a world—the antebellum North—that had seemed to conform in practice to this ideal. Most people worked for wages only for a while when young, eventually aspiring to own land or to run their own business. Republicans looked around them and saw a society in which wealth was relatively equally distributed and upward mobility was available to all who worked hard. A Northern man could profit from the fruits of his own labor, they thought, and because he was not dependent on anyone else, he had the integrity (or the "virtue," to use the language of Republicanism) to be entrusted with the vote. In this way a political and an economic understanding of society were completely intertwined. Freedom meant freedom from economic dependence as well as equal political rights.

In order to create exactly this kind of society in the South, Stevens wanted to give land to the freedmen. After all, only with a plot of land—"forty acres and a mule"—would freed slaves have the economic independence necessary for citizenship in a republic. This was a step too far for most Republicans, though, who worried about the assault on property rights that a large-scale redistribution of land would entail. Stevens and a few other radicals were lonely voices on this question. Instead, Congress concentrated on securing the equal political and civil rights of freedmen by passing the Fourteenth Amendment, which, when ratified by the states in 1868, defined U.S.

An engraving from *Harper's Weekly* (above) shows two very different groups of people celebrating the passage of the 1866 Civil Rights Act, which gave former slaves the basic rights of citizenship, including the right to serve on juries. On the left, blacks and wounded veterans cheer. On the right, respectable Washington ladies wave their handkerchiefs in celebration.

An 1889 cartoon by Joseph Keppler (below) shows the U.S. Senate in the grip of the robber barons. Anxiety about the rise of monopolies was becoming the central issue in American politics. Republicans were rightly seen as the pro-business party.

citizenship for the first time in a way that included black people. The Fifteenth Amendment, which was passed a couple of years later, made it unconstitutional for a state to abridge a citizen's right to vote on the grounds of race. By securing the principle of equal rights before the law, these hugely significant Reconstruction amendments, created and passed by Republicans, completely transformed the Constitution from an uneasy compromise with slavery into a powerful ally of all those who, over the next hundred years, would seek to realize the promise that all men are created equal. But securing equal political and civil rights was easier to do in theory than in practice. By rejecting Stevens's plea for land redistribution, Republicans denied blacks the economic independence that, before the war, most of them had thought essential for the maintenance of a free society.

In consequence, a new conception of freedom emerged during Reconstruction. It reflected a changing economic world. The largely classless republic of small farmers and artisans that Northerners had gone to war to preserve was being swept away by the development of capitalism. Wage labor was becoming the normal condition of working men. Freedom now meant freedom of contract, the right to leave one employer and to sign on with another. Equal political rights were the guarantor of that narrower conception of freedom.

In 1877, as the Republican Party finally gave up its efforts to secure the rights of freedmen in the South, a wave of industrial conflict swept the Northern states. A great railroad strike spread to other industries and began to cripple the economy. Employers hired gangs of armed men to force strikers back to work. Some Republicans, loyal to the old free labor ideal, supported the rights of labor. Most jumped the other way and supported the bosses who viewed labor unions as illegal organizations that restricted their freedom to maximize profits.

This new economic order, marked by huge rates of immigration and an increasing gap between the fabulously wealthy and a growing class of poor laborers, became known as the "Gilded Age," a phrase taken from the title of a novel by Mark Twain. Beneath a thin veneer of glittering extravagance, a tawdry and ragged society suffered the growing pains of capitalist development. In New York, the metropolitan center of the new prosperity, lavish parties and other exuberant displays of wealth were the symbol of the age. Mrs. Stuyvesant Fish once threw a dinner party to honor her dog, which arrived sporting a $15,000 diamond collar. The rich men who became known in the radical press as the "robber barons" captured the spirit of the age. Men like Cornelius Vanderbilt, Andrew Carnegie, and John D. Rockefeller made fortunes by consolidating huge monopolistic corporations that dominated industry. The antebellum world of small producers was long gone.

Most of this new elite was Republican. The party had no objection to individuals amassing great fortunes because Republicans believed that capitalism and freedom gave everyone the opportunity to succeed. They were optimistic about the future. The apotheosis of Republican hopes for national progress was the opening of the West to white settlement and agricultural development. In 1871 the Republicans ended the old policy of recognizing Indian tribes as sovereign powers and began to aggressively concentrate all tribes on Western reservations. This harsh policy culminated in 1876 in the famous battle of Little Big Horn, where General George Custer's small force was annihilated by Sioux warriors led by Chief Sitting Bull. Such uprisings dramatized the plight of Native Americans, but the only political consequence was to increase the congressional appropriation for the army. In return the new states in the West became reliably Republican, as they have remained for the most part.

The Republicans continued to be the party of moral progress, supporting the use of government to prevent vice and immorality, and the party of Protestantism, which meant they mistrusted the Catholic immigrants from Italy and Ireland. Above all, the Republicans retained the loyalty and support of many of those who had fought to defend the Union. Republican candidates "waved the bloody shirt" in election after election and propelled a series of Civil War generals to the White House: not just the hero, Grant, but Hayes, James G. Garfield, Chester A. Arthur, Benjamin Harrison, and William McKinley. Combining their moral, religious, and patriotic themes, Republicans condemned the Democrats as the party of "Rum, Romanism, and Rebellion."

While Republicans could always unite by attacking Democrats for their role in the Civil War, they were internally divided over the seemingly arcane issue of civil service reform. "Reformers" wanted to end the practice of giving government jobs to the supporters of the winning party. Their opponents, known as the "stalwarts" and led by Roscoe Conkling, a senator from New York, wanted to protect their right to appoint their friends to highly paid government jobs. This division had become acrimonious during the Hayes presidency and it dominated

A Republican elephant celebrates the election of Benjamin Harrison in 1888 in this *Harper's Weekly* cartoon.

OOSE."

the heated 1880 nominating convention. The eventual winner was the reformer James A. Garfield, who had not only the requisite war record but had also, like Lincoln, risen from a poor background. The stalwarts fumed at their defeat, and in order to appease them the convention selected Conkling's friend Chester A. Arthur as Garfield's running mate. The popular vote was almost a dead heat, but the Republicans won clearly in the electoral college. Almost immediately, however, the civil war in the Republican Party broke out again as President Garfield rejected Senator Conkling's choice for the plum position of New York's collector of customs. The dispute was unresolved when, barely four months into his term, Garfield was shot by a disappointed office-seeker. In the event, Arthur disappointed the stalwarts by endorsing a law that provided for competitive examination for federal jobs. On a personal note, Arthur restored some of the glamour that the White House had lacked under the temperant Hayes.

Between 1876 and 1892 the Republican and Democratic Parties were remarkably evenly balanced. Now that the Southern states once again had full representation in Congress, the Democrats tended to have a majority in the House, while Republicans had the edge in the Senate, thanks in part to the admission of a cluster of new states in the West. Because they did better in these small states, Republicans found it easier than Democrats to amass the electoral college votes necessary to win presidential elections, but these were always close. Twice, in 1884 and 1892, the Democrats won and put New Yorker Grover Cleveland in the White House.

By offering ever-increasing pensions to Union veterans and by never ceasing to remind voters of their role in saving the Union, the Republican Party reinforced its special relationship with the men in blue who had voted for Lincoln in 1864. However, the memory of the Civil War that was kept alive in successive Republican campaigns was one that was increasingly amnesiac about the great achievement of emancipation. As the years went by, Republicans no longer saw themselves as radicals. Admittedly, some old abolitionists continued to carry the torch of equal rights for blacks, but their voices became ever more lonely. The Republican faithful lost interest in the plight of the freedmen. Deprived of the vote, African Americans gradually lost the economic gains they had made during Reconstruction. As the great black leader W. E. B. Du Bois later wrote: "The slave went free; stood a brief moment in the sun; then moved back again toward slavery."

The Republican Elephant

This cartoon by Thomas Nast appeared in *Harper's Weekly* on November 7, 1874, and is the first to associate the Republican Party with an elephant. The inspiration for the animal scene was the Central Park menagerie scare of 1874. A hoax report had appeared in the *New York Herald* that there had been a mass breakout from the zoo, and that wild animals were roaming through Central Park. The *Herald* was, at the same time, accusing Republicans of "Caesarism" by floating the possibility of a third term for President Grant. The cartoon shows the *Herald* as a donkey wearing a lion skin—representing the prospect of Caesarism—scaring away the animals. The caption read: "An ass having put on a lion's skin roamed about in the forest and amused himself by frightening all the foolish animals he met within his wanderings." One of the foolish animals was the Republican vote, represented by the large, lumbering elephant, which was being scared away from its normal allegiance by the phony lion of Caesarism. It is heading into the hidden trap cunningly laid by the Democratic fox at the bottom of the picture.

The South in Ruins

The ruins of Richmond (top and right) after it was captured by the Union army in the spring of 1865. Much of the destruction was wrought by the Confederates themselves, who burned what they could before evacuating the city, as well as by Union shelling. Sherman's army destroys railroad tracks in Atlanta (above) in October 1864 before leaving for their infamous "March to the Sea." When the war was over, much of the

infrastructure of the South had been
destroyed, and much of the population
left destitute. This made the problem
of integrating freed slaves into
Southern society all the more difficult.

The Fifteenth Amendment

Reconstruction was a period of immense change in the social and political life of the South. Republicans in Congress guaranteed the equality of all citizens before the law, and former slaves began to shape their lives in a way that had never been possible before. Of all the revolutionary changes brought about by Reconstruction, none symbolized the defeat of the Confederacy and its old order so dramatically as black people voting and holding office—the fruits of the Fifteenth Amendment. This splendid print was produced in 1870 to celebrate the ratification of the amendment, which forbade state governments from denying the right to vote to any male citizen on the grounds of race. The images depict the advances in the status of African Americans since the end of the Civil War, including a black school and a black preacher giving a sermon.

EENTH AMENDMENT .

CELEBRATED MAY 19th 1870.

John R. Lynch was born a slave. He represented Mississippi in the U.S. House of Representatives for three terms and was the first black to deliver a keynote address to a major party's national convention.

Thomas Morris Chester was born free in Harrisburg, Pennsylvania. He was a war correspondent, and after training as a lawyer in England Chester was appointed a district superintendent of education in Louisiana.

Black Republicans

African Americans began to hold office in significant numbers in 1867, after Congress passed laws reorganizing Southern state governments and holding elections under franchise rules that did not discriminate on the basis of race. Over the next ten years—before the last of the Reconstruction governments were overthrown—more than 2,000 blacks held office at the federal, state, or local level. This was far from the "black domination" of later myth, but it certainly represented an enormous achievement. The number of African Americans in public office was not to rise to such high numbers again until the 1970s.

Robert Smalls, born a slave, went on to become one of the most influential Reconstruction politicians in his home state of South Carolina. He was elected to five terms in the U.S. House of Representatives.

Hiram Revels was the first black American elected to the Senate. Like many black officeholders, Revels was a minister in the African Methodist Episcopal church and had been an army chaplain during the war.

Frederick Douglass was an escaped slave who became a powerful spokesman for the abolitionist cause. Douglas continued to play an important public role during Reconstruction.

Reconstruction in practice: This poster (right) shows the radical members—both white and black—of the South Carolina legislature.

RADICAL MEMBERS
OF THE FIRST LEGISLATURE AFTER THE WAR

SOUTH CAROLINA

Dusenberry	Mayes	Demars	Rivers	Miteford	Smith	Swails
McKinlay	Jillson	Brodie	Duncan	White	Pettengill	Perrin
Dickson	Lomax	Hayes	BOOZER	Barton	Hyde	James
Wilder	Jackson	Cain	Smythe	Boston	Lee	Johnston
Hoyt	Thomas	Maxwell	Wright	Shrewsbury	Simonds	Wimbush
Randolph	Webb	Martin	MOSES	Mickey	Chesnut	Hayes
Harris	Bozeman	Cook	Sancho	Henderson	McDaniel	Farr
	Tomlinson	Miller	Sanders	Howell	Williams	Meade
	Wright *		Nuckles	Hayne	Gardner	Thompson
				Mobley		Rainey
				Hudson		
				Nash		
				Carmand		

* Afterwards associate Justice of the Supreme Court of the State

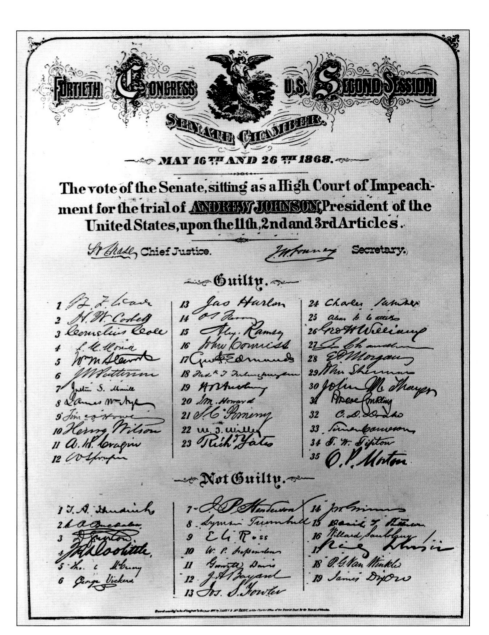

Impeachment of the President

Andrew Johnson (top left), the seventeenth president of the United States, was the first to be impeached. His relations with the Republican majority in Congress were tense because he habitually vetoed Reconstruction legislation. Radicals feared that unless Johnson were removed from office, Reconstruction would fail. The House "managers" (right) who presented the prosecution case to the Senate based their case on Johnson's alleged failure to uphold laws passed by Congress. As the certificate of the vote (above) shows, the vote to remove Johnson from office was 35–19 in favor, one short of the required two-thirds majority.

Grant for President

After the battle with Andrew Johnson, it was a relief to Republicans when Ulysses S. Grant (left) was elected president in 1868. Unfortunately, he proved to be much less successful as a chief executive than he had been as a general. His two terms in office were marred by scandals and the perception that he was not fully in control of his own administration. Vice President Schuyler Colfax (right) was tarnished by this perception of corruption when he became embroiled in the Credit Mobilier scandal. Republican congressman Oakes Ames had set up

the Credit Mobilier of America, a finance company designed to pluck profits from the government-financed building of the Union Pacific Railroad. In 1872 Ames was censured by Congress for having sold stock to a number of leading politicians, including Colfax, at much below their true value in order to create, as he later confessed, "a general favorable feeling" toward his complicated scheme. The financial markets were panicked by the scandal, and for a while leading investors in London boycotted American bonds.

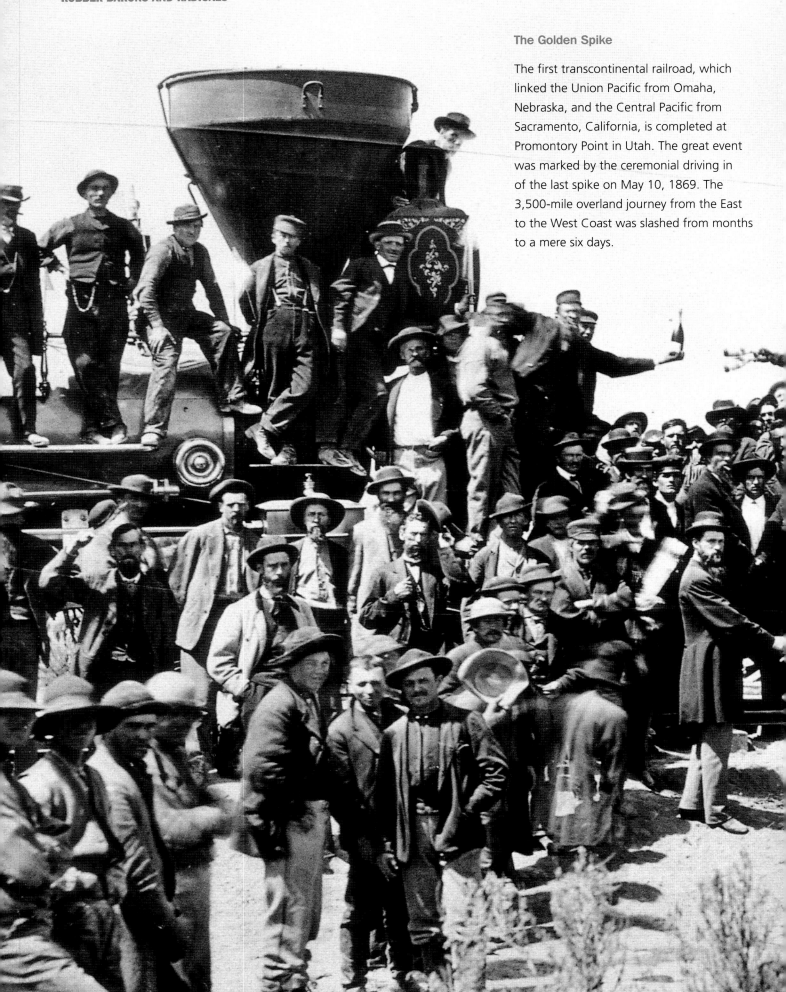

The Golden Spike

The first transcontinental railroad, which linked the Union Pacific from Omaha, Nebraska, and the Central Pacific from Sacramento, California, is completed at Promontory Point in Utah. The great event was marked by the ceremonial driving in of the last spike on May 10, 1869. The 3,500-mile overland journey from the East to the West Coast was slashed from months to a mere six days.

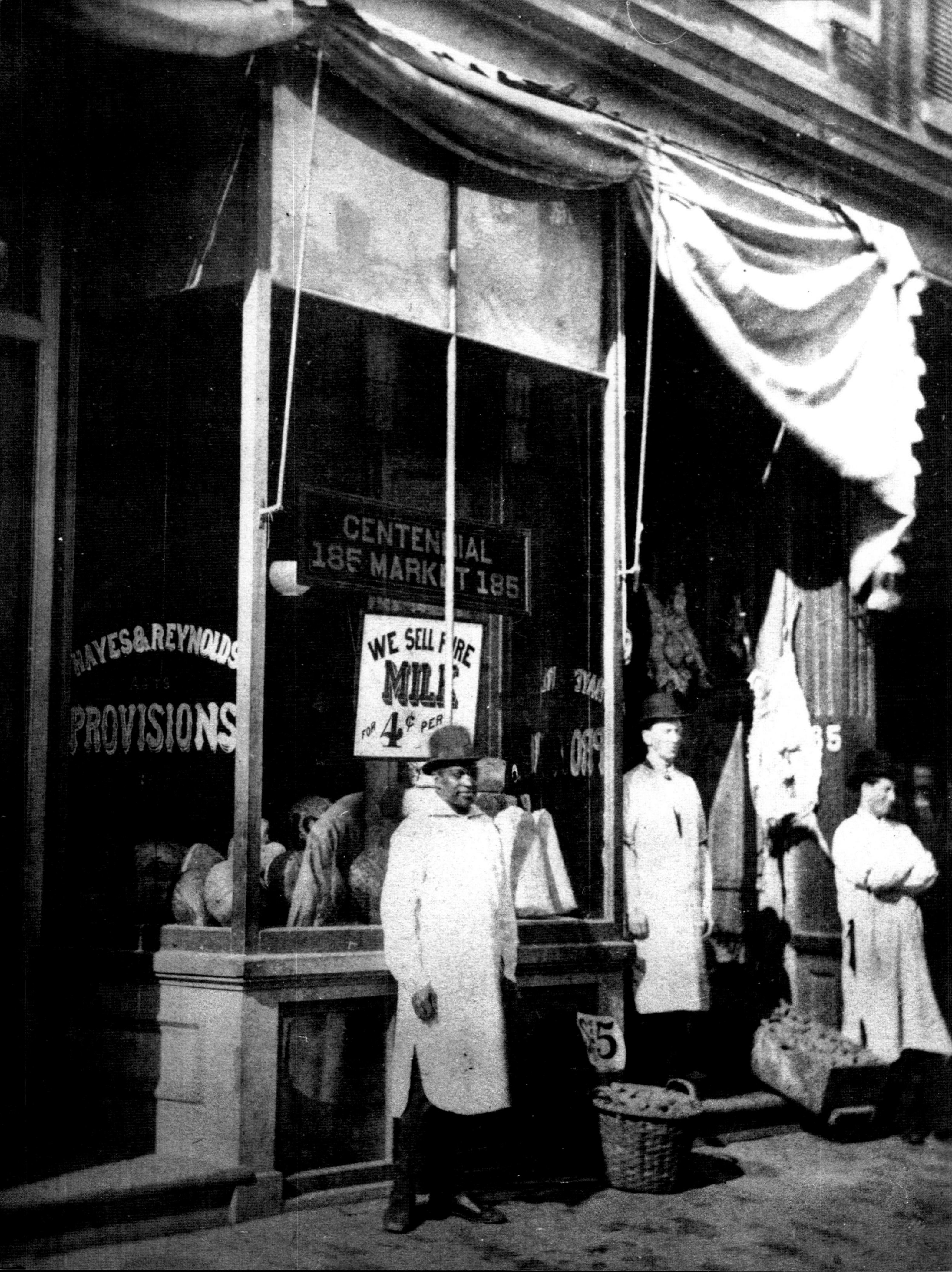
CENTENNIAL
185 MARKET 185
HAYES&REYNOLDS
PROVISIONS

The Unfinished Revolution

Republican Reconstruction legislation transformed the lives of blacks in the South. Their real income increased sharply in the decade following the end of slavery, while the average wealth of whites slightly declined. The African American photographed in front of his grocery store in 1876 (left) is emblematic of this progress. The Reconstruction acts and the Fourteenth Amendment to the Constitution guaranteed the civil rights of black Americans. The two images (this page) from Frank Leslie's *Illustrated Newspaper* show a lawyer addressing a mixed jury in a Southern courtroom, and blacks lining up to vote in Richmond, Virginia, in 1871. The depiction of the voter at the ballot box may seem rather condescending, but by the standards of nineteenth-

VIRGINIA.—CHARACTERISTIC SCENES AT THE SOUTH—NEGRO VOTING IN RICHMOND.—FROM A SKETCH BY WILLIAM L. SHEPPARD.—SEE PAGE 155.

century illustrations this is a remarkably positive depiction of African Americans. In their dress and in their deportment, they are the embodiment of respectability. Many of the political and economic gains made by blacks in the South after the Civil War were quickly eroded after 1877 when Democrats reclaimed control of all the former Confederate states.

Anything to Beat Grant

One of the strangest elections in
American history, the 1872 campaign
was a contest between President
Grant, fighting for a second term, and
Horace Greeley (right), the eccentric
editor of the *New York Tribune* and a
leading figure in Republican and Whig
politics since the 1840s. Greeley was
the candidate of the Liberal Republican
Party, a breakaway faction of
Republicans. As Reconstruction issues
faded in importance, the Liberals
identified the patronage system as
the source of inefficient and corrupt
government and attacked "Grantism,"
as they called the president's habit of
appointing cronies to plum positions.
They were also in favor of free trade,

the gold standard, and public education, and opposed to a continued military presence in the South. Although small in numbers, the Liberal Republican movement was extremely influential because it included leading editors and Republican politicians, including such radicals as Charles Sumner (left). Pessimistic about their chances of beating Grant on their own terms, Democrats also nominated Greeley. This created the peculiar situation in which the man who had been the scourge of Democrats all his political life was now spearheading their campaign to oust Grant, and the headquarters of the Democratic Tammany Hall machine in New York (far left) flew the Greeley banner. For all this, Grant was reelected by a landslide and Greeley died the day after the election, which meant that he received no votes when the electoral college met.

Inauguration Day, 1873

President Grant delivers his second inaugural address on March 4, 1873. He declared that he was committed to implementing, "so far as executive influence can avail," the civil rights of blacks. Social equality was a different matter, however. It was "not a subject to be legislated upon," Grant announced, and he pledged that he would not "ask that anything be done to advance the social status of the colored man, except to give him a fair chance to develop what there is good in him." Reconstruction was coming under heavy fire from liberal Republicans as well as from Democrats. In his second term, Grant became more and more reluctant to use federal power to enforce black rights in the South. Northerners were also becoming increasingly sympathetic to the white South as the rancor of the Civil War became a distant memory. Grant's pledge to aid the "restoration of good feeling between the different sections of our common country" was widely applauded. The former general also boasted of the small size of the federal army and navy, which was "less than that of any European power of any standing."

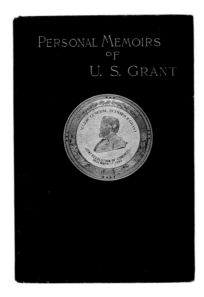

Grant's Last Days

The aging war hero and ex-president, photographed in 1884 working on his memoirs. He was now suffering from his final illness. Written with the help of Mark Twain, the memoirs were an instant best-seller, and they needed to be. Grant had been defrauded by a con man in 1884 and almost made bankrupt. The memoirs were insurance for his wife, Julia, and their children.

Mourning the Great Hero

The former president's death on July 23, 1885, prompted a wave of national mourning. Under the heading "A Hero Finds Rest," *The New York Times* reported that at the moment of the general's death, the sun dipped below a portrait of Lincoln on the general's bedroom wall. His body lay in state in New York City (right) and tens of thousands of people quietly filed past the coffin. In 1897 a spectacular memorial tomb in New York was opened (above right).

Freedmen's Bureau

A government agency established during the war to distribute food, medicine, and clothing to freed slaves, the Freedmen's Bureau played an important role during Reconstruction. As this sympathetic *Harper's Weekly* cartoon (right) shows, the bureau agent was the intermediary between the freedmen and often hostile white Southerners. Agents were usually former army officers and others with antislavery beliefs. Their difficult jobs included regulating labor contracts, adjudicating disputes, and running schools (above). A crowd gathers outside a bureau headquarters in Beaufort, South Carolina (opposite).

White Fear

John White Geary led a colorful life as a
Western adventurer and a Civil War
general. Although he had been a
Democrat before the war, he was the
Republican gubernatorial candidate in
Pennsylvania in 1866. This Democratic
poster (right) is attacking him for his
support of black suffrage. Black
delegates had indeed attended the state
Republican convention. Outrage at black
suffrage was much more intense in the
South. The illustration from *Harper's
Weekly* in 1867 (above) shows a black girl
being whipped by white Southerners
who accused her of not showing enough
respect. The Ku Klux Klan (opposite)
was only one of many clandestine
organizations that sprang up in the
postwar South to resist what Southerners
said was "black domination."

The Great Compromise of 1877

The election of 1876 ended in deadlock, with both candidates, the Republican Rutherford B. Hayes (above left) and the Democrat Samuel J. Tilden (below left) fighting for the electoral college votes of three Southern states where voter fraud and intimidation had been widespread. All across the South, Republican voters—mostly blacks—were prevented from getting to the polls. In the North, Republican state and city governments rounded up recent immigrants to prevent them from voting illegally (right). Hayes gained the prize after a congressional committee ruled by a strictly partisan vote in his favor. In return for gaining Democratic assent to the decision, Hayes immediately pulled federal troops out of the South and promised a "just and liberal" policy toward that region. This Republican cartoon from *Harper's Weekly* (above) depicts Hayes as he would like to be remembered, as the great conciliator between North and South.

American Dream—Indian Nightmare

This wagon train is bound for new lands in the Dakotas in 1885. In the thirty years after the Civil War, more land was settled and cultivated in North America than in the previous 250 years. And where these settlers went, the Republican Party followed. For the rest of the nineteenth and early twentieth century, the party could count on the votes of the new Western states. The price for this was paid by the Native Americans, who were forced onto reservations. When they rebelled, the response of the U.S. Army was uncompromising. In 1890 at Wounded Knee in South Dakota, more than 300 Sioux were killed. The photograph of U.S. Army officers and a civilian burial party (above) was taken two days after the massacre.

Foreign Influence

Republicans feared the social effects of the new urban slums, such as this one off Mulberry Street in New York (right). They also feared dangerous ideologies being imported into America from Europe, where socialism was on the rise, and they blamed immigrants for the increasing labor unrest. A strike arbitration committee (left) poses in front of a railroad car, while a Thomas Nast cartoon (above) shows an American worker being burdened by a foreign agitator. Children—most of whom are immigrants—are seen in a New York school saluting the flag and repeating the oath of allegiance (above left). Republicans repeatedly stressed the need for the rapid "Americanization" of immigrants and would have welcomed scenes like this.

Presidents Garfield and Arthur

Republican James A. Garfield was elected president in 1880, but had only been in office four months when he was assassinated (bottom right) in a Washington railroad station by Charles J. Guiteau, a mentally ill man who claimed he had been unfairly passed over for a federal office. The White House was draped in mourning after this shocking event (top right). Garfield was succeeded by Chester A. Arthur (above foreground), photographed here in 1882 during a camping trip in upstate New York.

"Little Ben" in the White House

Benjamin Harrison (above) won the Republican nomination in 1888 on the eighth ballot. He conducted one of the first "front porch" campaigns, delivering short speeches to delegations that visited him in Indianapolis. As he was only five feet six inches tall, Democrats dubbed him "Little Ben"; Republicans replied that he was big enough to wear the hat of his grandfather, "Old Tippecanoe," the Whig president William Henry Harrison. The Democratic candidate, Grover Cleveland, lost in the electoral college despite winning 100,000 more popular votes. Harrison was interested in foreign policy. He submitted a treaty to the Senate to annex Hawaii, but to his chagrin his Democratic successor, Cleveland, rejected it. Harrison was also the first president to visit the Far West while in office. He is pictured (opposite) visiting the Menlo Park home of Leland Stanford, the railroad entrepreneur who later founded Stanford University. On another occasion (above), Harrison poses with a number of Republican Party luminaries aboard a steamer in Maine.

The Gilded Age

The wealthy upper classes in late nineteenth-century America lived lives increasingly separated from the rest of society. The children of President and Mrs. Hayes are looked after by their nurse Winnie Monroe (left), while the Whitney home (far left) on Fifth Avenue in New York displays the opulence of the Victorian style. Wealthy New Yorkers (above) relax at a dinner, wearing crowns made of holly leaves.

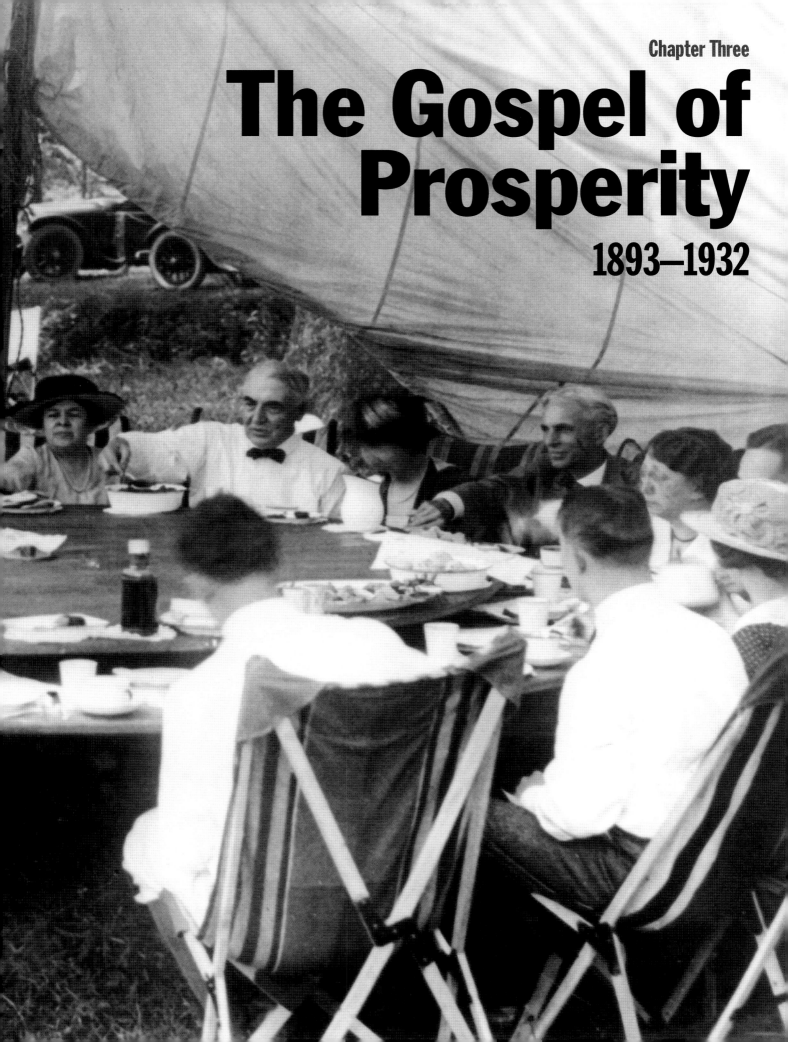

Chapter Three

The Gospel of Prosperity

1893–1932

The Gospel of Prosperity
1893–1932

I N 1893 A YOUNG HISTORIAN, Frederick Jackson Turner, captured the anxiety of a nation that was undergoing a fateful transition when he pointed out that, for the first time in American history, there was no more free land (meaning territory unsettled by whites) in the West. It was the existence of a continually expanding frontier that had made America different from Europe, Turner argued. In the West of the American imagination, all had the opportunity to succeed. Now that the frontier was closed, the United States would face the same problems as the Old World: class conflict and the vices of the cities. To Americans in 1893, Turner's words struck home because the prosperity they had enjoyed for the last two decades seemed to be coming to an abrupt end. A stock market crash caused nearly 500 banks to go bust. Industrial workers, if they still had jobs, saw their real wages fall by almost 25 percent in just two years. Lines of unemployed men filled soup kitchens in the big cities of the East, while Western farmers defaulted on their loans. These were hard times indeed, made worse by the increasingly urban and industrialized nature of American society.

Since the Civil War, elections had been closely fought. Although each party created caricatures of the other that were endlessly hawked around in campaigns, in truth, some of the most divisive economic and social issues cut across party lines. Easterners in both parties, for example, favored protective tariffs, while many Western farmers wanted lower tariffs to secure their growing export market in Europe. Monetary policy—especially the issue of whether the value of money should be based on the gold standard ("hard money") or on the freely available silver being mined in the West—also consumed political energies without clearly differentiating the parties. Most, but by no means all, Republicans favored high tariffs and hard money, but the Democrats were completely divided. Grover Cleveland, the Democrat who unhappily occupied the White House when the depression of 1893

Previous pages: President Harding (in center, serving himself salad) having dinner while on a "back to nature" camping expedition with leading businessmen and innovators Harvey Firestone (left foreground), Thomas Edison (being served by the waiter behind the tent pole), and Henry Ford (two to Harding's left).

Campaign poster for McKinley's reelection campaign in 1900— with the vigorous young Theodore Roosevelt as his running mate.

There were shocking scenes of poverty and squalor in big urban centers during the closing years of the nineteenth century. This photograph is from the famous series taken by Jacob Riis in New York City (Mulberry Street) around 1895.

struck, favored hard money and low tariffs. Much of his party vociferously disagreed. These issues, combined with popular frustration at the inability of the Democratic administration to offer any hope to struggling farmers and urban workers, caused political upheaval on an epic scale. In the midterm elections of 1894, Democrats lost more than half their seats in the House, some to the new Populist Party, but most to Republicans. By 1896 the Republican Party emerged as the dominant party in the nation, a position it was to retain until the the Great Depression came along in 1929. Between these two economic crises, Republicans offered Americans responsible government, social progress, and, above all, the prospect of material wealth. They preached a gospel of prosperity, and it brought them electoral wealth.

The election of 1896 turned out to be one of the most momentous in American history. The Republicans nominated William McKinley from the crucial electoral state of Ohio, and after a fierce battle over the platform, embraced the policy of high tariffs and hard money as the key to economic prosperity. Some Western Republicans bolted the party in disgust and joined the swelling chorus of Democrats and Populists who wanted their standard bearer in 1896 to champion the cause of silver coinage. Aggressively courting the distressed Western farmers and miners, the Democratic convention rejected the policies of the incumbent Democratic president, Grover Cleveland. The platform not only endorsed an unlimited supply of silver coinage but also attacked the use of legal injunctions and troops to put down strikes. Their candidate was the thirty-seven-year-old William Jennings Bryan, who had wooed the convention with a theatrical performance of his famous "Cross of Gold" speech. For the first time, partisan lines were clearly drawn on the major economic question of the day.

Attacking the dangerous radicalism of the Democrats and urging Americans to support conservative policies that would ensure economic prosperity, the Republican campaign struck chords that would bring them success time and again over the coming decades. In McKinley they had a candidate who was the personification of moderation, experience, and respectability. He was a warm and kindly man with striking, deep-set eyes and a handsome profile, and people instinctively trusted him. While giving the appearance of never actively seeking office, he astutely avoided making enemies by rarely saying anything of interest.

McKinley's victory was a watershed for the Republican Party. Bryan won all the Western states except Oregon, North Dakota, and California, but McKinley won every Northern state east of Wisconsin, which was more than enough to give the Republicans a comfortable majority in the electoral college. Although the Democrats retained strength in New York and Boston, the key to the new Republican majority was that they won all the other cities in the nation. In the years to come, Republicans forged an unbeatable coalition of city dwellers and upwardly mobile Midwestern farmers, which appeared to put the party on the side of history. It was in these years that the Republicans came to be known as the "Grand Old Party," or the "GOP" for short, a claim to longevity that was hardly deserved but which fitted with their self-image as the party of progress, respectability, and patriotism. An economic recovery shortly after McKinley took office only served to bolster the Republican cause.

In just three months, during the summer of 1898, the United States became a colonial power. McKinley was initially reluctant to intervene in the long-running Cuban war of independence from Spain, but the destruction of the USS *Maine* in Havana Harbor catapulted the nation into a quick and decisive war against the tottering Spanish empire. A few Republicans and many Democrats, including the irrepressible Bryan, were distraught by what they saw as the repudiation of the values of the old republic. But the war proved immensely popular with the public and made, in the process, the reputation of an energetic young New York Republican, Theodore Roosevelt, who resigned his post as assistant secretary of the navy in order to lead a volunteer cavalry company, which, with characteristic flair, he named the Rough Riders. Teddy Roosevelt was rarely out of the public eye for the next twenty years. On a wave of enthusiasm, he was nominated as McKinley's running mate in 1900, and the pair duly won a landslide victory against the hapless Bryan, who again was the Democratic Party nominee.

While McKinley kept a dignified presidential distance from the dirty business of campaigning, Roosevelt hurled himself into the 1900 race, making hundreds of "whistle-stop" speeches from the rear of a railroad car. With unflagging enthusiasm, he kept telling his spellbound audiences that they had a "full dinner pail" because there was a Republican in the White House, and he talked enthusiastically about the wonderful future that awaited America in the twentieth century.

Despite his popularity with the public, important interests within the Republican Party did not trust the young Roosevelt, and not merely because of his exuberant style. Wall Street bankers and self-made businessmen were angered by Roosevelt's opposition to "trusts" (as large corporations were then known), and by what they saw as his

The wreck of the USS *Maine* in Havana Harbor in 1898. The mysterious explosion that destroyed the vessel was blamed on the Spanish and became the excuse the U.S. needed to intervene in the Cuban war of independence.

A campaign prop from the 1900 election drives home the message that a vote for the Republicans is a vote for a "full dinner pail"—a variation on a familiar Republican refrain.

Clifford K. Berryman's cartoons (below) forever linked Teddy with bears; the connection has to do with an actual episode. At the end of an unsuccessful bear hunt in 1902, a tired old female bear was tied to a tree by the ranger so that the president could get his trophy. Roosevelt, being a true sportsman, declined.

idiosyncratic enthusiasm for conserving natural resources. It was New York City financiers and Republican Party bosses, irritated by Roosevelt's reformism during a short but eventful spell as governor of New York, who first suggested that he should become vice president—as a means of getting him out of their way. When McKinley became the third Republican president to be assassinated in just four decades, shot by an anarchist at the Pan-American Exposition in Buffalo just six months after his second inauguration, Roosevelt became, at the age of forty-two, the youngest-ever president of the United States.

Roosevelt was a new kind of Republican politician. His energy was boundless, his charisma an antidote to the succession of gray characters who had followed Lincoln. Few presidents enjoyed office as much. Despite his inherited wealth and Harvard education, Roosevelt had the magic touch that all politicians crave. People liked and trusted him, and so long as he remained in public life, his appeal was almost irresistible, not least because he was never afraid of controversial issues. If conservative Republicans hoped that in office Roosevelt would curb his trust-busting tendencies, they were to be disappointed. In the summer of 1902 the president toured the Midwest seeking public support for his strategy of actively using antitrust legislation to break up big monopolies. "We do not wish to destroy the corporations, but we do wish to make them serve the public good," he explained. Republicans were still the party of big business, but Roosevelt sought to demonstrate that capitalism would benefit ordinary Americans.

The early years of the twentieth century were the era of progressivism, in which reformers sought to abolish political corruption, make politics itself more democratic, and mobilize the resources of government to improve social and economic conditions. Although the Republican Party as a whole was still wary of active government, especially in economic policy, Roosevelt personified the restless search for solutions to problems. In his triumphal reelection campaign in 1904, Roosevelt campaigned on the slogan of a "fair deal," urging capitalists to be fair to the consumer as well as to their employees.

In Roosevelt's second term, the new "muckraking" press (a term the president himself coined) dug up a series of lurid scandals involving Republican businessmen buying legislators and stitching up deals to give themselves monopolies. Roosevelt determined to do something about it. Congress, though, was proving more and more resilient to the continuous stream of badgering special messages from the president— more than a hundred a year—that gushed up Pennsylvania Avenue from the White House. In 1906 Roosevelt even urged Congress to ban corporate contributions to political campaigns and to outlaw child labor. Never before had the nation seen a president so active in domestic policy. Roosevelt called the White House his "bully pulpit" and he relished every chance to preach. The public may have loved Teddy, but Republican leaders in Congress did not. In his final two years in office, Republican opposition halted the momentum of progressive reform. Needless to say, no campaign finance legislation was passed.

Having pledged not to seek a third term, Roosevelt left office with huge regret and with a withering parting blast at those in his own party, "the corrupt men of wealth," as he put it, whom he believed had sacrificed the interests of the ordinary people of America on the altar of their own insatiable material greed. As Roosevelt saw it now, Thaddeus Stevens, the radical Republican who had advocated land redistribution after the Civil War, had been right to fear that the development of capitalism would produce a class of poor laborers who could not exercise in practice the equal political rights they possessed in theory. Only a strong federal government, Roosevelt contended, could enable ordinary people to take a fair share of the enormous wealth being created by what was now the largest economy in the world.

Roosevelt was more in tune with the rest of his party when it came to his adventurous foreign policy. During his administration the navy was built up and U.S. influence in the Caribbean and the Pacific was aggressively extended. Setting a precedent for future interventions, the U.S. backed a group of Panamanian rebels who wanted to break away from Colombia, and in return took possession of a stretch of land through which they built the Panama Canal. Roosevelt was fond of quoting a West African proverb, "Speak softly and carry a big stick," and his "big stick" foreign policy formed a powerful part of his presidential image. Despite his well-deserved reputation for bellicosity, however, not all of Roosevelt's foreign policy initiatives were warlike. He was even awarded one of the earliest Nobel Peace Prizes in 1906 for intervening to negotiate a settlement in the Russo-Japanese War.

In these years the party of Lincoln began to lose its black support. Back in the 1890s President Benjamin Harrison had tried and failed to persuade Congress to enforce black suffrage in the South. But most Republicans, including Roosevelt, found it more expedient to acquiesce in the white South's imposition of Jim Crow segregation. In 1896 the Supreme Court ruled in *Plessy v. Ferguson* that segregation laws that

A 1908 campaign button for William Howard Taft, who became the twenty-seventh president of the United States. He later served a distinguished term as chief justice of the Supreme Court.

Unlike the more radical W. E. B. Du Bois, Booker T. Washington (above) was a spokesman for black Americans with whom whites felt comfortable. Washington focused on the need for black self-improvement, especially education, rather than pushing for political power.

This Clifford K. Berryman cartoon of the Progressive Republican, or Bull Moose, convention of 1912 mocks it as simply being a Teddy Roosevelt celebration party.

created "separate but equal" facilities for blacks and whites were entirely constitutional, the Fourteenth Amendment notwithstanding. Roosevelt, in truth, did not understand or take much interest in the South, but he was the first president since Lincoln to meet with an African American, Booker T. Washington, in the White House.

Roosevelt's handpicked successor, William Howard Taft, easily squashed yet another challenge by Bryan in 1908, and this large and amiable man, who had been a judge and an administrator but never before an elected politician, inherited the leadership of a Republican Party deeply riven between progressives and conservatives. Progressives like Senator Robert La Follette of Wisconsin pleaded for election reforms, including votes for women, and for a federal income tax that would equitably raise money that the government could spend on social improvements. These men fused a long Whig and Republican tradition of striving for moral improvement in society with a modern recognition of the need to adapt the old doctrines of economic laissez-faire to the realities of a complex industrial society. Progressives scored some notable successes under Taft, particularly the constitutional resolutions, later ratified as the Sixteenth and Seventeenth Amendments, which created a federal income tax and provided for the direct popular election of senators.

These issues divided the Republican Party down the middle. Conservatives opposed all measures that threatened to hamper the freedom of businesses to run their own affairs. Although Taft did make some effort to enforce the antitrust laws, conservatives regained control of the party after 1909, and the mantle of progressive reform passed to the Democrats, or more specifically to that wing of the Democratic Party represented by men like the new governor of New Jersey, Woodrow Wilson, a former history professor at Princeton.

Teddy Roosevelt, still the most popular man in America, was not about to let his progressive agenda die. Returning triumphantly from a hunting safari in Africa, he broke with his successor and, espousing ever more radical causes like workers' compensation laws, began to actively seek the 1912 Republican nomination. The conservative Republicans who supported the reelection of Taft beat off the Roosevelt challenge, and the ex-president and his supporters bolted the party, running instead as the Progressive Republican, or as it came to be known, the Bull Moose Party (after Roosevelt's cheery remark to reporters that he felt "as strong as a bull moose"). Democrats saw their chance to win at last and nominated Woodrow Wilson, who was as committed as Roosevelt to progressive reform, despite the fact that he led a party that had become increasingly restricted to the urban city bosses (hardly natural friends of democratic reform) and the South (where the problems of manufacturing industry were barely relevant). A divided Republican vote allowed Wilson to win one of the most tense elections for many years.

Wilson may have been close to Roosevelt on the key progressive causes, but when it came to foreign policy the two rivals could not, at first, have been further apart. When war began in Europe in 1914, Roosevelt campaigned tirelessly for American intervention, angrily accusing Wilson of being "yellow" in the 1916 election campaign and railing that the popular song "I Didn't Raise My Boy to Be a Soldier" was as laughable as singing "I didn't raise my daughter to be a mother." Wilson's proclamation of neutrality was an election-winner, though, and against a conservative Republican candidate, Charles Evans Hughes, he was comfortably reelected as the man who "kept us out of war." In truth, though, Wilson was moving cautiously toward involvement, and when the president loftily called the country to war in 1917 in order to force a "peace without victory," most Republicans supported him. When the war was over, many Republicans opposed Wilson's visionary postwar plans for a League of Nations. Senator Henry Cabot Lodge had been the leading Republican supporter of military intervention, but by 1919 he was articulating a deep and persistent strain of isolationism in American political culture. Wilson's plan was defeated and the League of Nations was established without the United States.

Republicans regained the White House in 1920 in a landslide. Their candidate, Warren G. Harding, a handsome Ohio senator, misread his speechwriter's plea for a return to "normality" during the 1920 election campaign and inadvertently coined a new word, "normalcy," which became the theme of the Republican administrations in the 1920s. Back in control of Congress, Republicans brought a halt to the Wilsonian reforms and established friendly relations between government and business. Two quintessentially Republican policies were implemented in these years. Prohibition, implemented in 1920, and immigration restriction (by the acts of 1921 and 1924) were the high tide of the moral reform impulse and the concern to protect Protestant values that had animated the first generation of Republicans more than half a century before.

The 1920s were the boom years before the fall. Although Harding remained personally popular, his administration was riddled with scandal and his death in 1923 provided the opportunity for a fresh start under

Crowds milling outside the New York Subtreasury (now Federal Hall National Memorial), across from the Wall Street Stock Exchange, in the dark days of October 1929.

Calvin Coolidge, who became famous for his epigrams such as "the business of America is business," which the voters thought made him sound profound. The sage and comedian Will Rogers summed up the administration pretty well when he said, "This guy Coolidge don't do nothin', which is just what the American people want him to do." The philosophy of the Republican Party in these years was to create the best possible environment in which businesses could thrive.

In the 1928 election the Republican banker Herbert Hoover won convincingly over the New York Catholic Al Smith, who campaigned to repeal Prohibition. The Republicans basked once more in a clean sweep of both houses of Congress and the White House. But unnoticed amid the celebrations, the 1928 election produced some ominous indications that the Republicans' hold over their Northern core vote was perhaps not as secure as it appeared; for the first time the Republicans won fewer votes than the Democrats in the nation's twelve largest cities. Combined with the solidity of the Catholic vote for Smith, this pushed Massachusetts and Rhode Island into the Democratic column for the first time since the Civil War. This loss of urban and Northeastern support was the quiet harbinger of a coming political revolution.

Hoover had not been long in the White House when the stock market crash of October 1929 brought the good times screeching to a halt and ushered in the Great Depression. Businesses failed and unemployment rose to 5 million in 1930, 9 million in 1931, and a horrifying 13 million as the election approached in 1932. This represented more than 10 percent of the entire population. Never before had the nation faced such a serious challenge to its faith in the capitalist system. It is not quite true that, as legend has it, Hoover did nothing. He held a series of conferences in the White House to which he invited business leaders and encouraged them to believe that good times would soon return. His optimism, though, was at odds with the reality that many Americans were facing. The hollow reality of poverty was sucking the life out of the Hoover administration. Many Americans blamed Hoover personally for their troubles. The shantytowns that sprung up on wasteland in the cities were known as "Hoovervilles"; "Hoover flags" were empty pockets turned inside out; "Hoover blankets" were newspapers used by the homeless to keep warm. Republicans had prospered when the economy prospered; now they were facing the whirlwind. The White House and Congress were there for the taking if only the Democrats could find the right candidate and a convincing message for a fearful nation.

A campaign button (left) for Harding and Coolidge in 1920. Harding had the advantage of coming from the electorally crucial state of Ohio, which, amazingly, was home to no fewer than seven of the eleven presidents elected between 1868 and 1920.

The Union Army Marches On

Parades of veterans marching in their old uniforms beneath tattered old battle flags were a common sight in Northern towns and cities between the Civil War and the turn of the century. This one took place in Washington, D.C., in 1902, when the veterans' organization, the Grand Army of the Republic, was still a powerful political force. Much more than simply a social club for old soldiers, the GAR offered a potent mix of nostalgia and hardheaded practical benefits. Annual encampments and reenactments of battles offered veterans the chance to relive the glory days of their youth. On a more practical note, the GAR built care homes, campaigned with great success for generous pensions for veterans and their widows, and, wherever they could, vigorously supported the Republican Party—the party that had saved the Union.

The Monied Metropolis

By the end of the nineteenth century, New York was the wealthiest city in the world. Since the Civil War, the U.S. had been transformed from a largely agricultural nation to the world's biggest industrial power. At the top of the pile was a new rich elite, with more money than the old aristocracy of Europe could dream of. On Fifth Avenue, between Fifty-seventh and Fifty-ninth Streets (above), expensively dressed men and women stroll in front of the Plaza Hotel, one of a new class of large hotels with private bathrooms and elevators that were the wonder of the world. In the luxurious antechamber of a Turkish bath in New York (right), pampering is the order of the day.

Domestic Virtues

While his opponent wore himself out tearing around the country making speeches, William McKinley ran what the newspapers called a "front porch" campaign in 1896 (above). Dining that year at the home of Mark Hanna (at the head of the table), one of the great political figures of the age, McKinley is sitting next to his wife, Ida Saxton. Ida and Will had fallen deeply in love when McKinley, returning from the Civil War, set up as a lawyer in Canton, Ohio, where Miss Saxton was the prettiest and best-connected young woman in town. But after the death of their two young children, Ida became prone to sudden fits, a shadow of her former self. McKinley always sat next to her at dinner so that he could throw a handkerchief over her face should she have a fit during the meal. Even in the White House, they appeared inseparable, sitting together at formal dinners in defiance of protocol.

NAVAL OFFICERS THINK THE MAINE WAS DESTROYED BY A SPANISH MINE.

George Eugene Bryson, the Journal's special correspondent at Havana, cables that it is the secret opinion of many Spaniards in the Cuban capital that the Maine was destroyed and 258 of her men killed by means of a submarine mine, or fixed torpedo. This is the opinion of several American naval authorities. The Spaniards, it is believed, arranged to have the Maine anchored over one of the harbor mines. Wires connected the mine with a magazine, and it is thought the explosion was caused by sending an electric current through the wire. If this can be proven, the brutal nature of the Spaniards will be shown by the fact that they waited to spring the mine until after all the men had retired for the night. The Maltese cross in the picture shows where the mine may have been fired.

Mine or a Sunken Torpedo Believed to Have Been the Weapon Used Against the American Man-of-War---Officers and Men Tell Thrilling Stories of Being Blown Into the Air Amid a Mass of Shattered Steel and Exploding Shells---Survivors Brought to Key West Scout the Idea of Accident---Spanish Officials Protest Too Much---Our Cabinet Orders a Searching Inquiry---Journal Sends

Remember the *Maine*!

The USS *Maine* is seen arriving in Havana Harbor for a goodwill visit in December 1897 (opposite top). When it blew up a couple of months later, killing over 250 American sailors, the reaction of the press made war with Spain inevitable. William Randolph Hearst's *New York Journal* (far left) led the cry for war, immediately jumping to the conclusion, as did Assistant Secretary of the Navy Teddy Roosevelt, that the Spanish must have been behind it. In fact, a 1970s investigation by the history division of the Navy Department concluded that the *Maine* was destroyed by 11,190 pounds of its own gunpowder, ignited by a coal bunker. The war against Spain made the U.S. an imperial power. American troops fought in the Philippines (above), which fell after Admiral George Dewey had destroyed the Spanish fleet in Manila Harbor. Dewey became a public hero and announced his candidacy for the Republican presidential nomination in 1900, but withdrew when the party bosses refused to back him. The American victory near Santiago in Cuba was much celebrated (left) and brought Roosevelt to the nation's attention—he had resigned his government position to lead his famous Rough Riders to triumph at San Juan Hill.

The Assassination of McKinley

The Pan-American Exposition in Buffalo in 1901 was a great celebration of American progress. On September 6, President McKinley arrived (left) and delivered a short speech to the crowd (above). Afterward, hundreds of people waited in line in the Temple of Music to shake hands with the popular president. The crowds were so packed together that it was hard for the president's three security men to scrutinize every outstretched hand, one of which belonged to Leon Czolgosz, an anarchist who had concealed a short-barreled revolver with a handkerchief. He fired two shots from close range, hitting the president in the pancreas. As McKinley fell to the ground he cried out, "My wife—be careful how you tell her! Oh, my wife!" The nation mourned the third Republican president to die at the hands of an assassin. Secretary of State John Hay, who had been private secretary to Abraham Lincoln, gave a moving eulogy before Congress (right).

The Grand Old Party

Aspen, Colorado, during the presidential election of 1900. Portraits of McKinley and Roosevelt adorn the clapboard storefront where the Republican Party had established its campaign headquarters. Party workers, a dog, and a crowd of curious boys pose for the camera. Colorado was a Democratic state in these years, as miners and some struggling farmers voted in large numbers for William Jennings Bryan. But the Republicans had the support of the more prosperous citizens: storekeepers, businessmen, and successful farmers. Becoming the nation's youngest-ever president after McKinley's assassination, Teddy Roosevelt was immensely popular. The campaign button (above) is from his victorious 1904 election campaign.

Steaming Ahead

While the nation's cities saw unprecedented industrialization, agriculture was also being revolutionized by new technology. In North Dakota in 1910, a Minneapolis Steamer pulls a John Deere plow in virgin sod (right). Ten years later, two men take a break from harvest beside a Republic truck in Fullerton, North Dakota. This was Republican country. The Dakotas, along with the Midwest, were booming farming areas until the 1920s, when a fall in wheat prices hit small farmers hard.

Lincoln's Legacy

The Republican Club of New York City holds its twenty-fourth annual Lincoln dinner, February 12, 1910. The spectacular display of flags on the back wall is adorned with the famous quote from Lincoln's second inaugural address. The wealthy diners may have each paid up to $100, which would have helped the party's election expenses. No women were invited. Lincoln's reputation was at its peak in these years. Most of the statues and memorials to the great savior of the Union that now exist were put up between 1900 and 1925, the grandest of which, Daniel Chester French's magnificent Lincoln Memorial, was unveiled in Washington, D.C., in 1922. February 12, Lincoln's birthday, was a holiday in many states. The Civil War was still recent enough history to be within the living memory of many people, but as the United States entered the twentieth century as the world's biggest economic power, the divisions and bitterness of the great conflict between the states seemed remote indeed. With Lincoln's reputation becoming more sanctified with the passage of time, Republicans did not lose the opportunity to remind voters at every election that they were the party of Lincoln. Loathed by many Republicans when he was alive, Lincoln's legacy won them many votes half a century later.

The Bully Pulpit

Previous pages: Election night in Herald Square, New York. A large crowd watches the results of the 1906 midterm elections, posted on huge boards as they came in by telegraph.

Unlike most of his predecessors since Lincoln, Teddy Roosevelt (above, with his family, and at right, giving a stump speech) saw the presidency as his chance to get things done and a place from which to preach about how things ought to be. He launched antitrust suits, regulated the meatpacking industry, expanded the national forests, called a White House

conference on corruption in college football, and in 1906, he ordered the Government Printing Office to use simplified spelling. Congress was not impressed with this last move, and Roosevelt later wrote to a friend: "I have succeeded in getting thru some things that I very much wisht although not always in the form I desired."

It was ironic that the most energetic and belligerent of American presidents should preside over a period of such international calm. That did not stop Teddy Roosevelt from having grand international ambitions for his country. When the government of Colombia refused to lease land in the northern province of Panama to the U.S., he sent gunboats to support a Panamanian "revolution" and took control of the thin strip of land on which a canal could be built. The first president ever to leave the U.S. while in office, Roosevelt went to inspect the works himself. He is seen here (right) pretending to drive a huge mechanical digger. In 1907 Roosevelt, who saw a looming conflict with Japan for control of the Pacific, sent a newly expanded U.S. Navy, dubbed the "Great White Fleet," on a worldwide trip as a demonstration of American military strength (left).

Taft's Turn in 1908

The 1908 Republican convention was held in the magnificent Coliseum Building in Chicago. Members of the public, including three elegantly attired young women (above), wait in line to enter the public gallery. Inside, Governor Charles S. Deneen of Illinois whispers conspiratorially with an unidentified delegate on the convention floor (below, on the left). Meanwhile in Cincinnati, Ohio, Fourth Street (left) is draped in flags and banners proclaiming support for Ohio's favorite son, William H. Taft, who later described his experience of campaigning as the "four most uncomfortable months of my life." Taft was widely seen as Roosevelt's favored candidate, and wags were heard to say that his name was an acronym for "Take advice from Theodore."

The Reluctant President

William Howard Taft (above, driving to his inauguration in the snow, and above right, speaking at a public meeting in Virginia in 1911) confessed that, as a lawyer who had never before held elected office, he felt like a "fish out of water." A rather comical image, perhaps, considering that Taft was so large that a new, specially made, large bathtub had to be installed in the White House so that the president, who weighed more than 300 pounds, could bathe. But if the president was never quite at ease, Helen Herron Taft—known to her adoring husband as Nellie—loved being first lady (below right). The garden party held to celebrate their silver wedding anniversary in 1911 was one of the most glamorous Washington had ever seen. Nellie left a permanent mark on the capital by requesting that Japanese cherry trees be planted around the tidal basin.

Always fascinated by the natural world, Roosevelt insisted that "we do not intend our natural resources to be exploited by the few against the interests of the many." He is seen here (top right) with John Muir, the great conservationist, on Glacier Point in Yosemite, California, during a trip to the West in 1903. Muir was a fellow enthusiast who argued that "God cannot save trees from man, only the government can do that," and Roosevelt duly persuaded Congress to create five national parks, 150 national forests, and fifty-one bird refuges. He had a very modern vision of the need to preserve nature for future generations. "The greatest good for the greatest number," Roosevelt wrote, "applies to the number within the womb of time." He was only fifty when he left the White House in 1909. In search of adventure, he went on a grand tour, game hunting in Africa (right) and traveling around Europe, including a meeting with Kaiser Wilhelm II of Germany (above). Several years later, when the kaiser's armies invaded Belgium and World War I broke out, Roosevelt took a belligerent anti-German stance. When the German ambassador in Washington reminded him of his friendly visit, he replied pointedly, "I will never forget the way His Majesty the emperor received me in Berlin, nor the way His Majesty King Albert received me in Brussels."

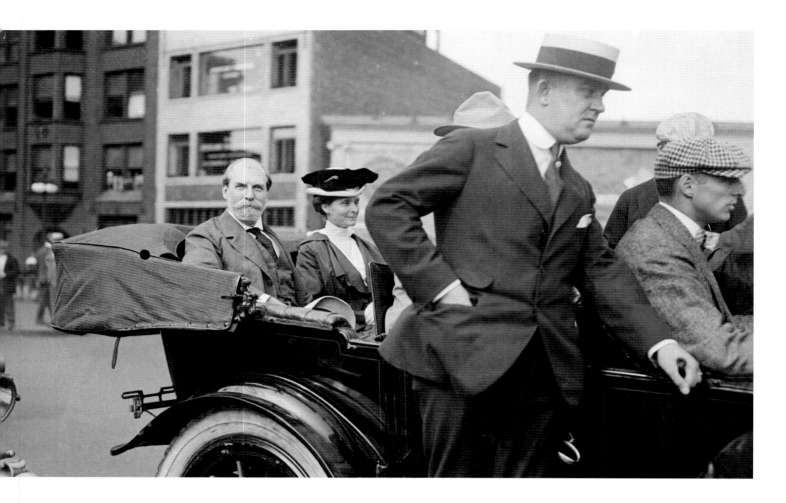

The Party Men

For over twenty years, the acerbic Boston Brahmin Henry Cabot Lodge (right) presided over Senate Republicans with a haughty grandeur. A man most comfortable in the cultivated company of writers like Henry James, he had little in common with the "Lion of Idaho," Senator William E. Borah (below, far left), an old-style progressive who often found himself isolated in an increasingly conservative party. But Borah remained optimistic, refusing to "accept the line of least resistance" and follow other progressives into the Democratic Party; he pledged to "make the Republican Party what it ought to be." Republicans of a very different stripe—loyal machine politicians Joseph G. Cannon of Illinois (House Speaker between 1903 and 1911) and Representative (later Senator) Theodore Burton of Ohio—confer at the 1908 convention (left). Charles Evans Hughes (top left) was the Republican candidate for president in the closely fought 1916 election against Woodrow Wilson. He famously went to bed thinking he had won and woke up to find he had lost. Later secretary of state under Harding and chief justice of the Supreme Court in the 1930s, he was the last bearded man to run for the presidency from a major party.

The Progressive Impulse

Progressivism was an amalgam of different reform impulses that shared the goal of abolishing political corruption and mobilizing the resources of government to improve social and economic conditions. During the presidency of Theodore Roosevelt, the Republican Party inspired the hopes of many progressives. Roosevelt refused to send in the army to break up a coal strike in 1902, instead forcing the mine owners to negotiate a settlement with the workers, whose wages were being cut and hours extended. Roosevelt also used his "bully pulpit" to highlight the plight of child labor and deaths from industrial accidents in the largely unregulated expansion of capitalism. Scenes like this of a boy who has lost his arm operating a saw in a box factory (far left), a child coal miner (left), and seven-year-olds operating dangerous factory machinery (right) aroused the sympathies of middle-class progressives. One of the most famous progressive campaigners, Jane Addams (above left), speaking to a crowd of reporters in 1915, was the founder of a settlement house in Chicago and later a peace campaigner and advocate of women's suffrage. Addams backed Teddy Roosevelt's Bull Moose campaign in 1912.

The divisions within the Republican Party between the progressives and the conservatives were brought into the open in the election of 1912. Roosevelt challenged Taft for the Republican nomination (left, the pair in more cordial times), and when that failed, his supporters bolted. In the fiercely fought three-horse race that followed (caricatured above right), Roosevelt's continuing popularity with the public was not enough to overcome the disadvantage of splitting the Republican vote (below right). Democrat Woodrow Wilson (far right) romped to victory echoing many of Roosevelt's progressive campaign themes.

Votes for Women

As the suffrage movement gathered momentum, it attracted ridicule. A group of young men gleefully rip up a suffrage banner outside the White House around 1914 (below). But Republicans in fact had a history of backing women's suffrage. The first legal women voters in America were in Republican territories and states in the West, and in 1917 Republican Jeanette Rankin of Montana (left) became the first woman elected to the House. The Nineteenth Amendment to the Constitution, which guaranteed women the vote across the nation, was ratified in 1920. In New York City in 1917, three women voters cast ballots (right).

The Height of Opulence

One of the world's richest men, banker J. P. Morgan proceeds majestically in his yacht *Corsair* down the lower East River, New York, in the 1920s. Powerful financiers like Morgan were at the apex of the prosperity promoted by Republicanism.

Frank W. Woolworth

Charles M. Schwab

George Eastman

John D. Rockefeller

Andrew Carnegie

George Westinghouse

The Money Men

In this great age of prosperity, a small number of entrepreneurs and innovators were able to amass incredible fortunes. Natural Republicans, these millionaires were, for obvious reasons, sympathetic to the idea that in the American system wealth denoted moral worth. Andrew Carnegie, owner of U.S. Steel, called it the "gospel of wealth." A great philanthropist, Carnegie believed it to be his duty to use his great fortune for the widest possible benefit. Other great magnates pictured here are J. P. Morgan, the banker and financier; George Eastman, the inventor of the Kodak camera; John D. Rockefeller, the founder of Standard Oil, the great monopoly to be broken up by the federal government under antitrust regulations; Henry Ford, the pioneer automobile maker; the splendidly mustachioed George Westinghouse, founder of the Westinghouse Electricity Company; William Boeing, airplane pioneer; Charles M. Schwab, steel magnate; Frank W. Woolworth, the grandest storekeeper in America; and Walter Chrysler, the innovative car manufacturer who built the beautiful skyscraper that bears his name.

Walter P. Chrysler

Henry Ford

J. Pierpont Morgan

William Boeing

Leading anglophile Republicans like Roosevelt and Lodge had been loudly advocating military support for Britain and France since at least 1915, and when President Wilson finally took the United States into the war in 1917, the nation was swept by a wave of patriotic euphoria. Hollywood had captivated America and new stars like Douglas Fairbanks helped to sell the war bonds known as "Liberty Loans" to finance the war (left). One of "Pershing's Doughboys" bids farewell to a loved one at the docks in New York (below left). A young woman poses prettily for a propaganda photograph while repairing army uniforms (below). American technology was an advantage in war as well as peace—one of the world's first tanks drives past the Flatiron Building in New York en route to Europe (right).

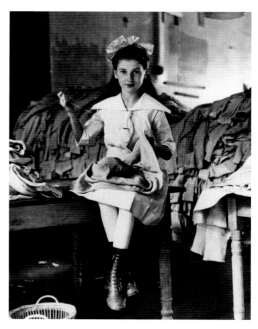

Celebrating Victory

On Fifth Avenue, New York, crowds celebrate Armistice Day, November 11, 1918, carrying allied and American flags (opposite, below). National Guardsmen who did not get to go overseas also celebrate (above) while demonstrating the effectiveness of the administration's deliberate anti-German propaganda.

German-Americans felt justifiably very vulnerable during the war, but not all went to the heroic lengths of air ace Eddie Rickenbacker to demonstrate their patriotism (top right). His daredevil exploits made him a celebrity at home, along with General Douglas MacArthur (right), America's most decorated soldier in the war.

Reaching for the Sky

A group of construction workers labor over the streets of New York, completing the construction of the Empire State Building in 1931.

Nothing symbolized the prosperity of the Republican years in the 1920s better than the building boom that transformed America's cities.

President's Picnic

Warren Gamaliel Harding was an astute politician who united the divided Republican Party and reassured the country that, after the trauma of war and the Red Scare that followed, life would now return to what he called "normalcy." With a disarming capacity for self-deprecation and with none of the intellectual weight of his predecessor, Harding nevertheless liked to surround himself with talented people. He is seen here at a rural retreat with Henry Ford and Thomas Edison (right, Ford on the extreme left with Edison beside him); with Albert Einstein and Sigmund Freud (below left, Freud on the president's left, Einstein on his right); and on a fishing trip (below right).

Triumph of the Drys

In 1920 the Twentieth Amendment to the Constitution was finally passed, prohibiting the sale or consumption of alcohol in the United States. This was a very Republican measure, the kind of moral reform that had been supported by crusading Protestant evangelicals since the 1850s. Few of those early prohibitionists had been quite so militant as the fearsome, six-foot-tall Carrie Nation (above), who between 1900 and her death in 1911 smashed up saloons and liquor stores all over America with stones, billiard balls, and a hatchet. U.S. Customs officials destroy liquor at the Brownsville Customs House, Texas, in 1920 (left). But in those parts of the country where the population did not favor it, the measure proved impossible to enforce properly, and the "noble experiment" failed in its objectives.

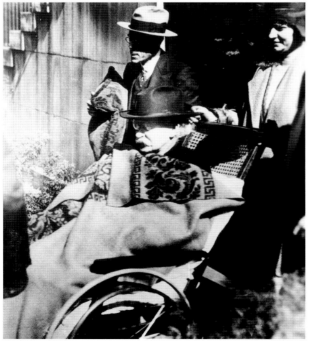

Ending on a Sour Note

Toward the end, the Harding administration was rocked by a series of financial scandals. Attorney General Harry M. Daugherty, an old Harding crony, was at the center of the most serious of them—the memorably named Teapot Dome scandal. A Berryman cartoon from 1924 (left) shows a teapot-shaped steamroller of scandal about to squash Daugherty and Secretary of the Interior Albert B.

Fall, who were both accused of profiting from selling off government-owned oil wells, the most notorious of which was called Teapot Dome. Fall (far left, at his trial in a wheelchair) was found guilty and jailed, but Daugherty (top left, talking to the press) was acquitted, possibly by bribing the jury. When asked in a 1926 interview whether he was the most maligned man in America or its

cleverest crook, he simply smiled and replied, "You can take your choice." Just as the crisis was breaking, Harding died suddenly in August 1923 and was deeply mourned by the nation (above). However, in a sense his death was timely for the Republicans, since it enabled Vice President Calvin Coolidge, who was not implicated in any way, to lead the party to victory in the election the following year.

Time for Enjoyment

The 1920s witnessed a boom in leisure activities, a trend that was greatly accelerated by the omnipresence of the automobile. On the July Fourth weekend in 1925, the beach at Nantasket, Massachusetts (right), is jam-packed with people—and the nearly identical-looking cars that brought them there. It was also a great decade for sport: Republican congressmen Herbert W. Taylor of New Jersey and Albert H. Vestal of Indiana are seen enjoying the golf links at Chevy Chase, Maryland (above).

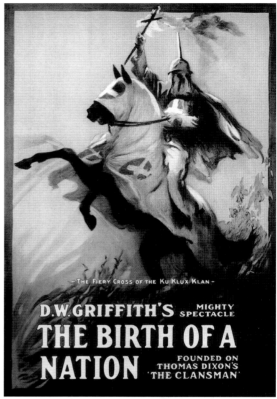

Racial Politics

During World War I and its aftermath there was a rise in racial tension in America. The National Association for the Advancement of Colored People marches down New York's Fifth Avenue in 1917 (right), protesting violence against blacks. Partly inspired by the 1915 film *The Birth of a Nation*, which presented a blatantly distorted view of Reconstruction, the Ku Klux Klan was revived in the 1920s and is seen here marching through the nation's capital in 1926 (left). Despite their proud history as the party that was created to stop the spread of slavery, most Republicans did not take a stand against racism in the 1920s, and black support for the party began to ebb away as a consequence.

The Coolidge Era

Calvin Coolidge, the former governor of Massachusetts, became president when Harding died of a heart attack in 1923. He was reelected in 1924 with a snappy campaign song called "Keep Cool and Keep Coolidge." "If you don't say anything, you won't be called on to repeat it" was Coolidge's considered observation of the perils of political leadership, but in fact his many aphorisms, such as "the business of America is business," effectively captured the spirit of his approach to politics, which was to let the country run itself. This was music to the ears of groups like the Republican Businessmen's Association of New York, cheering the president and first lady (above). A little less in his element, perhaps, the president meets with a delegation of Sioux (above right). Nearing the end of his tenure in 1928, Coolidge has a chat (right) with the Republican nominee for president that year, Herbert Hoover, a popular banker who promised to continue Republican prosperity into the 1930s.

Bonus Marchers and Hoovervilles

The Great Depression that followed the stock market crash of 1929 wiped out the savings and took away the jobs of millions of Americans. In 1932 thousands of World War I veterans who had fallen on hard times and called themselves the "Bonus Army" marched to Washington to demand early payment of the cash bonuses that a grateful Congress had promised to pay them in 1945 (left). A bill to pay the bonuses passed in the House against the opposition of Republicans loyal to Hoover, who wanted to maintain a balanced budget and so objected to the $2 billion cost. The Senate rejected the bill two days later, prompting the Bonus Army to shuffle up and down in front of the Capitol for three days in what newspapers described as a "death march." Meanwhile, two young residents of one of the shantytowns that became known as "Hoovervilles" sit by signs that make clear who they blame for their plight (above).

Chapter Four

The Long Road Back

1932–1968

The Long Road Back
1932–1968

THE BLUE-BLOODED, Harvard-educated Franklin D. Roosevelt had much in common with his distant cousin Theodore. Both were bursting with energy and ambition, both had a natural ability to connect with people from all walks of life, and both were convinced that an active government could be a force for social good. But the fact that the younger man had chosen to become a Democrat rather than a Republican reflected a significant change in American politics. For the first half century of its existence, the Republicans had been the party of hope and progress, the Democrats the party of memory and conservatism. By the time Franklin Roosevelt entered political life, that was no longer true. Under Woodrow Wilson, the Democrats took up the challenge of creating a legislative and governmental framework that could regulate the new industrial capitalism. The years of prosperity in the 1920s had sapped much of the progressive spirit in the Republican Party, while the Democrats had shown a new hunger to improve the lot of ordinary people. Under Harding, Coolidge, and Hoover, Republicans had become more than ever the defenders of the status quo, the party of laissez-faire.

The Great Depression made such rigidity seem callous. In the election of 1932, a seismic shift in political loyalties took place that made the Republicans the minority party for the next four decades. Democrats forged a coalition between the South, the working class and immigrant vote in big Northern cities, and for the first time, many poor Western farmers. They also won the battle of ideas. The New Deal offered a sense of purpose to which Republicans had no answer. FDR explained his aim in words that could have been spoken by Theodore Roosevelt: "To preserve we had to reform." Reform, guided by a group of young intellectuals with a commitment to social justice, meant embracing the power of government in the service of economic recovery.

In the face of the political energies unleashed by the New Deal, the Republican Party sunk in a few short years from a position of dominance to a bickering minority. Throughout the 1930s, almost

Making good use of the distinctive Republican elephant, this button from the 1932 election promises recovery if Hoover is reelected.

Previous pages: Former general Dwight D. Eisenhower, his wife, Mamie, and the thirty-nine-year-old Richard Nixon with his wife, Pat, in celebratory mood. The scene is the platform of the Republican National Convention in Chicago, July 1952, after they were nominated for president and vice president, respectively.

The Republican campaign in 1936 departed from the conventional red, white, and blue color scheme and made extensive use of this sunflower symbol. Democrats responded with the slogan "Sunflowers Die in November"—and sure enough, Alfred M. Landon was defeated in a landslide.

When government in the shape of the New Deal was offering so much, the Republican message fell on deaf ears. The party's fortunes reached their nadir in the 1936 elections.

everything the party did seemed as if it were calculated to alienate the broad mass of voters on whom they had previously been able to count. Some Republicans recognized the futility of flatly opposing such popular policies. Senators William Borah, Gerald Nye, and Hiram Johnson, for example, all progressive veterans of the Bull Moose campaign of 1912, were happy to accept the New Deal principle of governmental responsibility—even while criticizing the inefficiency of its implementation and the recklessness of deficit financing. These men had, after all, always seen themselves as the representatives of the little man. Nye even attacked Roosevelt for favoring Big Business while neglecting farmers and small businessmen. Borah supported the Louisiana populist Huey P. Long's "Share Our Wealth" plan, a scheme in the old populist tradition that advocated high taxes, government welfare, and debtor relief in order to benefit the poor.

Noisy as these old-time progressives may have been, the dominant faction within the party were conservatives like former president Hoover, who condemned New Deal programs outright as unconstitutional and dangerous. The public was not in a mood to listen. In the 1934 midterm elections, the Republicans lost even more congressional seats and state houses than they had two years earlier. In 1936 the progressives managed to prevent a group of stubborn conservatives from renominating Hoover. Instead, the Republican candidate was the genial Kansas governor Alfred M. Landon, who cautiously endorsed some New Deal programs while attacking Roosevelt for his autocratic style. Landon suffered a humiliating defeat, losing every state but Maine and Vermont, while in Congress Republicans slipped to their lowest ever ebb; only eighty-nine of them faced a phalanx of 331 Democrats. Never since the party's founding had Republicans looked so irrelevant to national political debate.

All factions within the party could unite in heartily opposing Roosevelt's high-handed attempt in 1937 to outmaneuver the conservative Supreme Court—which had been blocking key New Deal legislation—by appointing additional justices. The Court-packing plan, as it was known, had the added benefit, from the Republican point of view, of dividing the Democrats. As the New Deal coalition began to show signs of stress, Republicans restored some pride by making important gains in the 1938 midterm elections. By this stage, the New Deal reforms were making enemies in the business community while farmers were resenting the "straitjacket" of regulation in which they found themselves.

Facing the prospect of a third term for FDR, Republicans turned in 1940 to Wendell Willkie, a man who as recently as 1936 had been a registered Democrat. Willkie was a corporate lawyer who had gained a national following after some charming and fluent performances on radio talk shows, but he was a complete political novice, having never before run for office or held any public position. He had the great advantage, however, of being supported by Henry Luce, owner of *Fortune* and *Time* magazines. Accompanied by cries of "We want Willkie," this unlikely outsider stormed the Republican convention much to the disquiet of the party leadership.

Willkie ran a spirited but chaotic campaign. Much to the frustration of party leaders, he never concealed the tenuousness of his Republican allegiance, referring in speeches to "you Republicans" rather than "we Republicans." Willkie consolidated the Republican heartlands in the Midwest but could not come anywhere near matching Roosevelt's huge popularity. His attempts to portray himself as a man of the people caused New Dealer Harold Ickes to acidly describe him as "that simple barefoot Wall Street lawyer."

Along with some moderate criticism of the New Deal, Willkie began the campaign by endorsing Roosevelt's policy of lending arms and supplies to Britain, which was under sustained nightly attack from German bombers. As the election drew nearer, however, Republican Party leaders persuaded Willkie to change tack and pledge that as president he "would not send one American boy into the shambles of another war." In doing so, Willkie found belated favor with the Republican rank and file, which had become deeply isolationist. Isolationism was a powerful impulse in a nation that felt removed from the destructive squabbles of the Old World. In the mid-1930s, Senator Gerald Nye led a special investigation into the role of arms contractors in leading the United States into World War I. The influence of the Nye Commission report was such that by 1939, the majority of the Republican Party in Congress were not only strongly opposed to military "preparedness," but found themselves in the curious position of popularizing the socialist doctrine that wars are fomented by an international capitalist conspiracy. The small towns and farms of the Republican heartland in the Midwest and the prairie states where this near-pacifism was strongest encouraged a folksy conservative populism that was deeply suspicious of business and government alike. Driven by pressure from this rural Western Republican faction, the 1940 platform committee very nearly included a plank condemning

The Willkie campaign is represented in this striking image as a phoenix rising from the ashes. Sadly for the GOP, this was not what happened.

With his trademark wave of his hat, Wendell Willkie arrives at the University of Wisconsin, Madison, during his enthusiastic but unsuccessful 1940 campaign.

Jeanette Rankin, the first woman to be elected to Congress, was a lifelong peace activist. In 1941 she was the only member of Congress to vote against the declaration of war against Japan after Pearl Harbor.

The Republican ticket for 1948 paired the 1944 presidential candidate, Thomas Dewey of New York, with California governor Earl Warren.

World War I as a failure. While Willkie echoed the president's support for Britain "short of war," other Republicans formed America First, an isolationist pressure group that was very strong in the Midwest. High-profile supporters included senators like Gerald Nye as well as the dashing Colonel Charles Lindbergh, who in 1927 had captivated the world and become a national hero with the first solo nonstop flight across the Atlantic Ocean.

When, after the Japanese attack on Pearl Harbor in December 1941, President Roosevelt finally took the United States into the war, most of the Republican Party fell into line behind him immediately. The lone dissenter in Congress opposing the war resolutions was Republican Jeanette Rankin, who back in 1916 had been the first woman to be elected to the House of Representatives. While Republicans joined in a bipartisan support for war measures, they nevertheless capitalized on public discontent at government price-fixing and rationing and continued with their long-standing attacks on the centralizing and inefficient New Deal bureaucracy. In November 1942 Republicans made substantial gains in Congress and were, from this point on, able to frustrate and even reverse key New Deal measures.

The most spectacular Republican gain in the 1942 elections was the victory of Thomas E. Dewey in the race to become governor of New York. Dewey was a public prosecutor who had attracted national fame for his dramatic crusade against organized crime. With the support of the party hierarchy, he won the presidential nomination in 1944 with ease, and in normal circumstances would have been a formidable contender. As the Allies advanced victoriously across Europe, however, voters' memories of Republican isolationism made Dewey's campaign a difficult one. There were few subjects that it was safe for him to discuss. He attacked the administration for being staffed by "tired old men" and made other similarly veiled references to the president's failing health. Dewey's running mate, Senator John Bricker, was less restrained, playing to the Right and accusing Roosevelt of being under the influence of Communists. Nothing, though, could stop the reelection of Roosevelt for an unprecedented fourth term. Once again the Democrats carried all the large cities and industrial states. Republicans polled well among Midwestern farmers and in small towns outside the South. The administration clearly had the advantage of incumbency in wartime, but it was still hard to escape the conclusion that the New Deal had consolidated the Democratic loyalties of what seemed to be an unshakably large majority of American voters. Only a profound shift in the issue orientation of American politics could revive GOP fortunes.

Roosevelt's death in April 1945 brought a temporary partisan truce. Republicans rallied to help the hitherto obscure Missouri politician Harry S. Truman end the war. It was in this context that, despite much private unhappiness, most Republicans supported the establishment of the United Nations and approved the Marshall Plan, which gave millions of dollars of aid to the war-ravaged countries of Europe. Soon afterward, though, Republicans were working hard to capitalize on public discontent with the long Democratic incumbency, with frustration at the continuation of wartime price controls into peacetime. Republicans argued that prosperity would return only if the economy was freed up. Aided by the bumper-sticker slogan, "Had Enough? Vote Republican," these midterm elections were, at long last, a triumph. The party gained a majority in both houses of Congress for the first time since 1928.

In 1948 there was a fight in the Republican convention for a nomination that many observers really believed would select the nation's next president. Conservatives favored the man known as "Mr. Republican," Senator Robert A. Taft of Ohio, the son of former president William Howard Taft, who had first made his name as a pro-business foe of the New Deal. The nomination went instead, once again, to the more liberal Dewey. Not surprisingly, given his liberal credentials as a highly competent and moderate governor of New York, Dewey picked up support in the big cities in the East on a scale not seen since the 1920s. He failed, though, to break the Democratic hold on organized labor and the ethnic vote. In the closest election for years, Truman scraped home, but not before an early edition of the *Chicago Tribune* made the notorious blunder of running the banner headline "Dewey Defeats Truman."

The New Deal coalition persisted, but cracks were clearly discernible beneath its surface. Truman alienated Southern Democrats by ordering full racial integration in the armed forces—ending the segregated black units that had existed right through World War II. When the president then insisted on a civil rights plank in his 1948 platform, determined white supremacists, or Dixiecrats, bolted and nominated South Carolina governor Strom Thurmond as their candidate. Running an openly racist campaign, Thurmond began the

Thomas E. Dewey was defeated in 1944 by Roosevelt and in 1948—in one of the closest elections in American history—by an elated Harry S. Truman. Dewey went to bed on election night thinking he had won—as did the *Chicago Daily Tribune*!

Robert Taft failed in three bids for the Republican nomination—for the last time here in 1952, despite being presented with a Democratic donkey.

process of luring away conservative white Southerners from their hitherto rock-solid loyalty to the Democratic Party. It took two more decades before the process was complete, but it was Thurmond and his fellow Dixiecrats who first breached the dam that would later transform the American political landscape.

In retrospect, 1946 to 1948 was a watershed for the Republican Party, most obviously because it marked the beginning of the end of their years in the political wilderness, but also because it was a time of transition. The old "farm bloc" progressives were dying or losing power. The Taft-Hartley Labor Relations Act of 1947, which sought to reduce the power of unions, set the tone for a return to a pro-business agenda. When a leading Republican explained to a Senate committee in 1952 that, "What is good for the country is good for General Motors, and what's good for General Motors is good for the country," the phrase seemed to encapsulate the new Republican worldview.

Fast disappearing in this new postwar world was the isolationism of the 1930s. For Americans, the cultural impact of the cold war was acute. Suddenly and for the first time, Americans lost their sense of invulnerability. The Atlantic Ocean was no barrier against nuclear war. Freshmen congressmen like Richard Nixon of California were coming of political age in a climate shaped not by the Great Depression but by the anxieties of the early cold war. The United States was now acknowledged as the leader of the free world against the emerging Communist threat in an era shaped by the fear of nuclear Armageddon. Intervention in foreign lands and the building of a powerful military, both of which would have been anathema to a previous generation, now became a moral duty.

In this alarming new world, Republicans who had been warning for years about the Communist menace had fresh evidence to fuel their anxieties. Events in Europe and Asia in the late 1940s and early 1950s convinced many Americans that the Soviet Union was bent on world domination. Truman was attacked for the "loss of China" and was compelled to send U.S. forces to South Korea to defend the pro-Western government against Communist invaders from North Korea, backed by the People's Republic of China. At home, Congressman Nixon made his name by spectacularly accusing Alger Hiss, a prominent New Dealer, of being a Soviet spy. For years conservative Republicans had been claiming that the New Deal was part of a Communist plot, but until the Hiss trial—which ended in his conviction for perjury—such claims had appeared ludicrous. Nixon got good political mileage out of anti-Communism. He became a senator in 1950, smearing his opponent—the glamorous New Dealer Helen Gheghan Douglas—as a Communist sympathizer, and in 1952 was selected as the party's vice presidential candidate.

More than any other figure, Senator Joe McCarthy gave a brief flurry of hope to the Right in the early 1950s. He came to personify the crusade to expose Communist subversives in the government and the armed forces as well. Although many senior figures in the party establishment were embarrassed by the Wisconsin senator's wild language and shameless demagoguery, McCarthy, from a working-class Catholic background, nevertheless resonated with many ordinary Americans. Adroitly, he played on popular resentments against Eastern liberal elites. "It is not the less fortunate, or members of minority groups who have been selling this nation out," he told an audience in Wheeling, West Virginia, "but rather those who have had all the benefits the wealthiest nation on Earth has to offer. . . . This is glaringly true of the State Department. There the bright young men who are born with silver spoons in their mouth are the ones who have been the worst." Many were willing to go along with that.

McCarthyism did not break the New Deal coalition. Democrats and Republicans were not sufficiently differentiated on foreign policy questions for that to happen. It did, however, lay down important markers for the future. Between 1950, when he made an electrifying speech in which he had brandished a supposed list of Communist subversives in the State Department, and 1954, when his fellow senators finally turned against him, McCarthy shone a piercing political light on an important vein of working-class conservatism within the Democratic Party. Just like Southern whites, these people still linked their economic fate to the Democratic Party because of the material benefits they had gained from the New Deal, but they never really signed up to the liberal political project. A road map for a new populist conservatism for the cold war era was beginning to emerge.

In 1953 twenty years of Democratic occupation of the White House finally came to an end. General Dwight D. Eisenhower, or "Ike" as he was affectionately known, was a war hero who was trusted by voters to stand up for American interests abroad. He was also a moderate on the domestic issues that still divided the parties. Democrats could split their tickets and vote for Ike without challenging the essential elements

General Dwight D. Eisenhower, supreme commander of the Allied Forces during the Normandy landings in 1944. Eisenhower followed generals Washington, Jackson, and Grant from battlefield success to the White House.

of the New Deal settlement. The Republicans did win small majorities in both houses of Congress in 1952, but in 1954 the Democrats took power on Capitol Hill, once again demonstrating the continuing commitment of most voters to the liberal agenda of using an activist government to stimulate growth and aid social progress. Eisenhower liked to consider himself above mere partisanship. His low-key style of governing, which involved long hours on the golf course, was well suited to an increasingly prosperous and confident decade. As the columnist Richard L. Strout observed, "The less he does the more they love him. He is the man who doesn't rock the boat."

In contrast to Truman, Eisenhower showed little commitment to civil rights. Since the New Deal, more than 80 percent of blacks who were able to vote supported the Democrats. The party of Lincoln was no longer the party of black Americans. The president inadvertently advanced the civil rights cause in his first year of office, however, by appointing the former governor of California and Republican vice presidential candidate, Earl Warren, as chief justice of the Supreme Court. Less than a year after his appointment, in a unanimous decision, the Court ordered the desegregation of public schools with "all deliberate speed" in the landmark *Brown v. Board of Education* case, opening the way for the transformation of Southern race relations.

Many Republicans harbored reservations about what they felt was an unwarranted extension of government power into people's private lives. Eisenhower spoke for many in his party (and outside it) when he observed, "I don't believe you can change the hearts of men with laws or decisions." But the president ultimately defended the right of the Court to lay down the law and sent troops into Little Rock, Arkansas, to implement the Court-mandated desegregation of Central High School in the face of opposition by Governor Orval Faubus and mobs of angry whites.

In 1956 Eisenhower won a comfortable second election victory over the brainy patrician Adlai Stevenson in a replay of the 1952 contest. Television came into its own in the campaign for the first time this year. The old-style stump oratory had had its day, and a new era of media politics was beginning.

Rejecting Truman's policy of sending food and economic aid to third-world countries caught between the two cold war blocs, Eisenhower sent arms instead. As a fiscal conservative, though, Eisenhower tried to keep a control on the expansion of the defense budget. He saw nuclear weapons as an effective way of deterring the

It was not just martial glory that underlay Eisenhower's popularity, but a genial and trustworthy public image that was captured brilliantly by one of the pithiest and most memorable campaign slogans ever—"I like Ike."

Soviets, which, in the words of Defense Secretary Charles E. Wilson, delivered "more bang for the buck." The CIA was a relatively cheap foreign policy tool, and the agency ran covert operations that overthrew a popularly elected Guatemalan leader and helped the shah topple a nationalist government in Iran and establish a repressive but pro-American regime in its place. With delicate understatement, Eisenhower wrote privately in 1955 that "our traditional ideas of international sportsmanship are scarcely applicable in the morass in which the world now flounders."

Perhaps this comment was symptomatic of Eisenhower's unease at the political consequences of America's new global role. The old republic, the world of Lincoln and Teddy Roosevelt, removed from the "entangling alliances" of the Old World had, in a very short space of time, become the biggest military power the world had ever seen. By the time Eisenhower left office in 1961, the U.S. military had bases on every continent, and more than three and a half million Americans were employed in the military or the arms industry. In his televised farewell address to the American people, Eisenhower warned of the consequences for the values of the republic. "An immense military establishment, new in the American experience . . . is felt in every city, every statehouse, every office of the federal government," he warned. "The potential for the disastrous rise of misplaced power exists and will persist. . . . Only an alert and knowledgeable citizenry can compel the proper machinery of defense with our peaceful methods and goals, so that security and liberty may prosper together."

Vice President Richard Nixon—despised by the liberal wing of the Republican Party but adored by conservatives—lined himself up to succeed Eisenhower in 1960. His Democratic opponent was the glamorous Massachusetts senator John F. Kennedy. In a desperately close race, Nixon's defeat has often been put down to his pale, sweaty, and uncomfortable appearance in a TV debate against the tanned, relaxed Kennedy. Crucial votes may also have been decided by the way in which the two candidates responded to the arrest of civil rights leader Martin Luther King Jr. in Atlanta for trying to sit at a whites-only lunch counter. Nixon distanced himself from the controversy, while Kennedy intervened with important Georgia Democrats and King was released on bail. Whatever the deciding factor, Kennedy won with a margin of only 0.2 percent of the popular vote. Republicans had felt that their star was in the ascendant, but by the narrowest of

In 1960 Nixon's campaign contrasted his eight years as vice president with the relative inexperience of Senator John F. Kennedy of Massachusetts.

Image is everything: Radio listeners thought Nixon won the crucial first debate with JFK, while TV viewers came to the opposite conclusion.

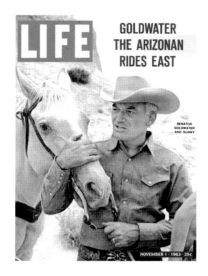

This *Life* magazine cover from November 1, 1963, carries a striking photograph of Senator Barry Goldwater. The next year, the darling of the Republican Right secured the Republican presidential nomination, but went down to heavy defeat at the hands of LBJ.

margins, and almost certainly with some fraudulent manipulation by Democratic bosses in Illinois and Texas, they were once again relegated to minority status. As the dour Nixon retreated into a failed and bad-tempered race for the California governorship, the 1960s seemed to promise a new liberal dawn.

After the tragic killing of President Kennedy, Republicans confronted a Southern Democrat in the White House who was serious about civil rights. As Lyndon Johnson signed the 1964 Civil Rights Act into law over the bitter opposition of Southern Democrats, he told a friend, "I think we just delivered the South to the Republican Party."

Just as they had in the first years of the New Deal, Republicans responded to the liberal energy of Johnson's Great Society by moving further to the right. In 1964 the party nominated Barry Goldwater from Arizona, who more than lived up to his promise to be a "choice, not an echo." His defense of states' rights came from a Jeffersonian fear of federal power, not from a racist ideology, but in the context of the racial politics of the 1960s, this distinction did not matter. Goldwater had been one of only eight senators who had voted against the Civil Rights Act of 1964, and it was in 1964 that the Republicans first made serious inroads in the South, winning support from whites in all income groups. Nevertheless, Johnson was elected by a landslide, winning 61 percent of the popular vote, the biggest margin since Roosevelt's crushing 1936 victory over Landon.

Democrats celebrated what seemed to be a resounding endorsement of Johnson's liberal big government agenda and a scathing repudiation of Goldwater's brand of conservatism. But this was to be the high-water mark of the liberal ascendance. For Republicans, whose hopes of recovery had been raised and dashed before, this, finally, was the darkest hour before the brightest dawn.

Determined to avoid the accusation of being "soft on Communism" that had dogged Truman, the Johnson administration poured troops into Vietnam to fight the Communist forces of Ho Chi Minh. Once again Republicans found themselves having to deal with a Democratic administration at war. This time, though, the war was deeply controversial and seemingly unwinnable.

Between 1964 and 1968 liberalism was being pulled apart by the centrifugal forces of antiwar protest, white backlash, and a slowing economy. It was nearly four decades since the Republicans had been the dominant party, but the stage was now set for a pivotal political moment as momentous as that of 1932.

FDR (above, with family, in the year he took office) proved to be one of the most remarkable political leaders of all time. With his personality and his New Deal policies, he established a rapport with the American people that the Republicans could not seriously challenge. The National Recovery Administration was a New Deal agency designed to stabilize and revive the nation's economy by drawing up industrywide codes that set standards for production, prices, and wages. It was launched in 1933 in a blaze of publicity (above right). Initially welcomed by both labor leaders and businessmen, it soon came under fire when it became clear that big corporations were ignoring the provisions that protected labor, while companies resented the agency's bureaucratic complexity. The cartoon (right) satirizes FDR as a rather hopeless quack who is treating Uncle Sam with an endless assortment of medicines in the hope that something will work. Conservative Republicans such as former president Hoover attacked the New Deal in much harsher terms as an unconstitutional extension of government power. It was certainly the most dramatic shift in the relationship between the government and the people since the Civil War, and it profoundly altered the party's political landscape as a result.

Voices of Protest

Huey Long, Frances Townsend, and Father Charles Coughlin captured the anxious spirit of millions of Americans during the 1930s who worried about the concentrations of power and the erosion of community. Long (above) called for a new federal plan to redistribute wealth, while Coughlin (left), in weekly radio broadcasts, lambasted the New Deal for not being radical enough. His newspaper *Social Justice* (right) became increasingly anti-Semitic and anti-Communist in the late 1930s. Meanwhile, Townsend called for a pension of $200 a month to be paid to every American over sixty "on condition they spend the money as they get it." The result, Townsend claimed, would be to pump money into the economy and create new jobs for younger people. The plan captured the public imagination (placard, above right).

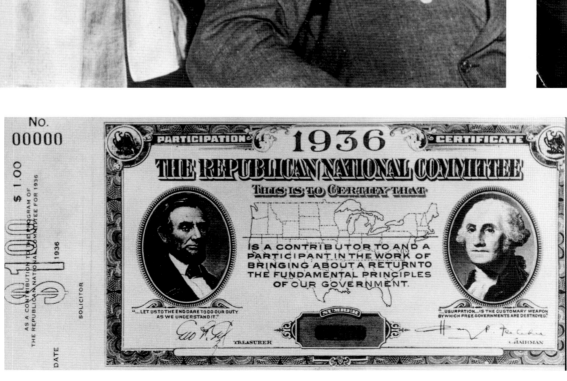

The Roosevelt Landslide

With the jaunty campaign song "Happy Days Are Here Again," FDR was reelected in 1936 by a landslide with the enthusiastic support of a coalition of Western and Southern farmers, industrial workers, urban ethnic voters, reform-minded intellectuals, and African Americans. In an era before reliable opinion polls, this result was unexpected. Indeed, *The Literary Digest* had conducted a very unscientific survey that had predicted a big win for the Republican candidate, Kansas governor Alfred M. Landon (above left with FDR and, in the background, future president Harry S. Truman). Republicans had even, with unjustified overconfidence, adopted the slogan "Make it a Landon-slide." Eighty percent of newspapers and even some conservative Democrats, like former presidential candidate Al Smith, endorsed Landon, who campaigned against the centralization of the New Deal. The GOP raised campaign funds by selling "certificates" to supporters for a dollar. This one (left) follows a familiar Republican theme by linking the GOP campaign to the fundamental values of the republic and the iconic figures of Lincoln and Washington. Election day brought the novelty of mechanized voting machines for these New York voters (above).

Elephant at the Ball

On February 7, 1940, at the Annual Grand Ball of the New York Republican Party, a group of young women appear with the emblem of the party—an elephant. The photograph captures the feel of the exclusive Eastern elites who were an important element in the party in this period. New York Republicans managed to elect Thomas Dewey to the governorship in 1942. The elephant, meanwhile, has been an amazingly durable symbol. Ever since its first appearance in a Thomas Nast cartoon after the Civil War, Republicans have embraced the image because of its connotations of strength and purpose and because it is distinctive and instantly recognizable.

Putting America First

An influential body of Republicans, especially the farm bloc from the Midwest and the prairie states, were strongly isolationist. In July 1940, just weeks after the fall of France and with Britain under nightly bombardment from the Luftwaffe, the America First Committee was formed to keep the U.S. out of the war. A few America Firsters were openly supportive of the Nazis but most simply argued that intervention would be useless. They wanted to protect American values at home, not by fighting foreign wars. Isolationists included Republican and independent senators Henrik Shipstead, Arthur H. Vandenberg, Robert La Follette Jr., Hiram W. Johnson, and William E. Borah, seen here at a 1939 session of the Senate Foreign Relations Committee (below left, sitting left to right). America First's most noted spokesman, though, was the former aviator Charles Lindbergh, who, despite his increasingly anti-Semitic rhetoric, attracted a large following (right, speaking in Chicago in April 1941). Within a year America First had set up more than 450 chapters and regularly held large rallies such as the one (above left) at New York's Madison Square Garden on October 30, 1941.

"We Want Willkie"

In 1940 Republicans turned to Wendell Willkie, who ran a spirited, if sometimes disorganized, campaign under the banner of "Progress and Prosperity." A former Democrat, Willkie criticized the New Deal for its inefficiencies but did not propose to abolish it completely. His campaign pitch was essentially that the Republicans were due for a spell in office, and was summed up in the slightly risqué slogan "No man is good three times." The Roosevelt camp replied with the succinct "Better a third-termer than a third-rater." Willkie had an ebullient personality that went down well on the campaign trail. He is seen here arriving in Chicago, greeted by huge, cheering crowds (right), and in Lansing, Michigan, on September 28, 1940 (above left), where he made a speech vigorously denouncing the claim of Governor Herbert Lehman of New York that a defeat for Roosevelt would be a victory for the fascist dictators. In Willkie's hometown of Elwood, Indiana (below left), enthusiasm for the local favorite has spilled over into the streets.

Previous pages: These Walt Sanders photographs show young Willkie supporters setting out to woo the voters in October 1940.

Defeated Yet Again

Willkie was initially the front-runner for the Republican nomination in 1944, but in the end the party turned to a more conventional choice—the governor of New York, Thomas E. Dewey. He faced the immense challenge of conducting a campaign in the midst of a war against an incumbent commander in chief. Dewey's most effective strategy was to emphasize his youth and energy, which contrasted with Roosevelt's increasingly obvious frailty. He also insinuated that the Democratic campaign was being indirectly financed by Communists through their domination of the Congress of Industrial Organizations (CIO), a big donor to the Democratic Party. Dewey is pictured (left) after his acceptance speech in Chicago on June 28, 1944. Some of his supporters (plus a stuffed Republican elephant) pose for the press photographers (top right). Dewey's supporters had hoped that the other rising star in the party, the liberal Republican California governor Earl Warren, later chief justice of the Supreme Court, would agree to be the running mate, but Warren declined and the nomination went to John W. Bricker of Ohio. Warren is pictured (below right) during his successful gubernatorial election campaign in 1942 on the back of his campaign train, together with yet another Republican elephant.

Republicans at War

Just as in the years after the Civil War, politicians metaphorically—and sometimes literally—paraded in front of the electorate in their wartime uniform. So, after World War II, a politician's war record could be his ticket to success. None had a reputation to match Dwight D. Eisenhower, whose image is painted on the fuselage of this USAAF bomber (left). A future generation of Republican presidents in more lowly military capacities are Naval Lieutenant Richard Nixon, in the Pacific in 1944 (right, helmeted), and Naval Aviator George H. W. Bush (below left), who was shot down over the Pacific on September 2, 1944, and later awarded a Distinguished Flying Cross for his bravery. Ronald Reagan (below right, with his mother, Nellie) served in the army reserves and made training films. At the end of the war, he was discharged with the rank of captain.

End of an Era

Henrik Shipstead was one of the leading figures in the Minnesota Farmer-Labor Party, which capitalized on the discontent of urban workers and poor farmers who felt that the New Deal was taking power out of the hands of local communities. He entered the U.S. Senate in 1923, where he was allied to farm bloc Republicans. In 1940 Shipstead formally changed his affiliation to Republican and was reelected for a fourth term. Shipstead and other old-line progressives like Gerald Nye, William Borah, and Robert La Follete Jr., had been an important, if minority, voice during the New Deal years, but by 1946 their politics seemed antiquated and irrelevant. Here Shipstead stumps at Cottonwood in the 1946 primary campaign (left), listened to by three members of his natural constituency (above). He went down to defeat. In the chill of the cold war, Republicans were turning increasingly to the rhetoric of anti-Communism, which would launch the national career of Wisconsin senator Joseph R. McCarthy (facing camera), seen here eating chicken on Lincoln's birthday in 1951 with fellow senators Butler (center) and Wherry.

Mixed Fortunes in 1948

Republicans finally regained control of Congress in 1946 and were confident of victory in the race for the White House in 1948. At the Republican National Convention in Philadelphia in August, two black delegates wear Dewey buttons (right). These Southern delegates were probably photographed precisely because they were unusual. Many African Americans had deserted the GOP during the New Deal and would continue to be staunch Democrats over the coming decades. President Truman's insistence that a civil rights plank be incorporated into the 1948 platform was one of the factors that led to the creation of the breakaway States' Rights Democratic Party, whose candidate was South Carolina Governor Strom Thurmond (far left, being dressed by his black valet in 1947). The agonizingly close election night was covered for the first time on TV (left, the ABC studios). Although Dewey narrowly lost to Truman, the election did see the emergence of several future Republican stars, including Gerald Ford (above left) of Michigan.

HUAC, Hollywood, and Hiss

Freshman congressman Richard Nixon (far right) made his name by taking a lead role on the House Un-American Activities Committee. FBI chief J. Edgar Hoover (above left, testifying on March 26, 1947) was a strong supporter of the committee's investigations into suspected Communist infiltration of the government. In 1947 the movie actor Robert Taylor (above right) was one of several "friendly witnesses" called to testify before the committee on the extent of Communist infiltration of Hollywood. But the most celebrated case pursued by Nixon was against the former State

Department official Alger Hiss, an educated, handsome New Dealer (above left, taking the oath in August 1948). Whittaker Chambers, a former Communist, testified in December 1948 that Hiss had turned over top-secret government documents to the Soviet Union. Although he was convicted of perjury in 1950, Hiss always protested his innocence and repeatedly tried to clear his name. Many Americans believed him, some accusing the FBI of fabricating evidence. Soviet files opened up in 1995, however, strongly suggested that Hiss had been guilty after all.

Reds Under Beds

Although his name has become shorthand for political smearing, Senator Joe McCarthy was as much a product of the paranoid political climate as the instigator of it. Some of the worst excesses of the Red Scare—such as the firing of public school teachers for suspect political views—continued for years after his power was broken. His downfall was hastened by the 1954 investigation into alleged Communist infiltration of the armed services. McCarthy is seen here talking to his lawyer, Roy Cohn (left), at a tense moment. The McCarthy hearings with the army revealed the senator's bullying tactics and reckless innuendos to a huge television audience, such as this group intently watching the hearings in New York (below). Some of the most heated exchanges took place between McCarthy and Joseph Welch, the lawyer representing the army. The moment that most shocked the viewers was when Welch exclaimed, "Have you no sense of decency, sir? At long last, have you left no sense of decency?" McCarthy just shrugged, but many applauded someone who at long last was prepared to stand up to him. In December 1954 McCarthy was censured by fellow senators. He died three years later at the age of forty-eight, a broken man.

Hats Off for Ike

The party's isolationist, Midwestern Main Street tradition was kept alive after World War II by Senator Robert A. Taft of Ohio, who sought the GOP nomination for president in 1944, 1948, and 1952. Despite coming into the 1952 convention in Chicago with the greatest number of delegates (left), Taft was once again defeated by the party's Eastern establishment, although this time by a candidate who went on to win the White House. The New York delegation reserved its seats on the convention floor with a clear indication of where their loyalties lay (right). Although Taft was first in the hearts of most of the dedicated Republicans in the convention hall, they were also desperate to pick a winner after twenty years out of office. Since only a third of the nation's registered voters were Republicans, the party had to find a candidate who could appeal to Democrats and independents as well. Ike was that man—not only because he was a war hero, but also because he embodied a new spirit of moderation in the party. He won with 55 percent of the popular vote. His coattails were not long, though. Republicans did win back control of both houses of Congress but only by the most slender of margins, which disappeared in 1954.

The Power of Television

General Eisenhower, his wife Mamie beside him, rides in triumph through the streets of Chicago (opposite). The most difficult moment of the campaign for the Republicans was when it was revealed that wealthy Californians had set up an illegal "slush fund" for Ike's running mate, Richard M. Nixon. GOP leaders considered dumping him from the ticket, but Nixon brilliantly used a TV address (top) to his advantage, claiming that the only gift he had received was a little puppy that his daughters had named Checkers—and he certainly was not going to give that back! Television was now the principal medium of the campaign and was creating new public figures like the first great TV anchor, Walter Cronkite (above). On election night, CBS sensationally used a computer to accurately predict the winner.

War in Korea

American troops, with UN backing, had intervened in Korea in 1950 to prevent a Communist takeover. The decision to commit U.S. forces had been President Truman's alone, which meant that the president was politically vulnerable when initial American success was reversed by the intervention of Communist China. Truman began to seek a negotiated settlement and was forced to fire his brilliant and obstinate commander, General Douglas MacArthur, who argued in a well-publicized letter that "there is no substitute for victory." Public protests in support of the general further weakened the president's authority (above left). MacArthur was briefly touted for the Republican nomination, but the winner—that other World War II hero, Eisenhower—clinched victory with a campaign pledge that if elected he would go to Korea and end the stalemated war. He is pictured here in an army jeep near the front line on December 4, 1952 (below left). Marilyn Monroe (right) raises morale among U.S. servicemen in Korea in 1954. The war was over by this time, having cost more than 50,000 American lives, but troops remained—part of the ever-expanding U.S. military presence around the globe during the cold war.

Confronting Communism

Madame Chiang Kai Shek, the wife of the Chinese Nationalist leader, was a great celebrity in 1950s America. During World War II, she had played a major role in gathering international support for the Chinese Nationalists, and in 1943 she had even addressed a joint session of Congress. After the Communist victory over Chiang's Nationalists in 1949, Madame Chiang was exiled to Taiwan with her husband but continued to make frequent visits to the United States. A charming and charismatic figure, she became the embodiment of resolute anti-Communism, and her presence and public popularity made any suggestion of normalizing relations with the People's Republic of China politically unacceptable. She is pictured with President Eisenhower at the White House in 1953 (above). One of her leading supporters, Secretary of State John Foster Dulles (left, relaxing on a trip to Southeast Asia), played a leading role in shaping U.S. foreign policy until his death in 1959.

They Still Like Ike

The 1956 election was a rerun of 1952. The Democrats, ever optimistic, renominated Adlai Stevenson, who had lost so overwhelmingly four years earlier. The GOP met in the convention hall of San Francisco's Cow Palace and renominated Eisenhower and Nixon by acclamation. At a campaign rally in Madison Square Garden in New York (left), the Republican faithful keep their eyes peeled for the appearance of their hero.

A Winning Combination

The Eisenhower-Nixon ticket in 1956 went into the election
campaign as overwhelming favorites to repeat the 1952 GOP
victory. At a rally in Madison Square Garden in New York, a
supporter (left) displays what she thinks of Ike's opponent.
Eisenhower left much of the energetic campaigning to Nixon,
seen here riding through Evanston, Illinois (top left), and
speaking to a rally in Oakland, California (far left). "Ike and
Dick" won over 57 percent of the popular vote, the biggest
tally for the GOP in a presidential election since Warren
G. Harding crushed James M. Cox in 1920.

Display of Strength

President Eisenhower (right, campaigning in the Midwest in 1952) presided over a massive buildup of the U.S. military. Although the Republican Party had always opposed the expansion of the size of government, under Eisenhower the federal government assumed an ever larger share of national spending, mostly through huge increases in the military budget. In the 1957 inaugural parade, the latest weapons are displayed before the president and vice president (left), as is a more symbolic form of strength—a Republican elephant.

The Joys of Consumerism

With the expansion of consumer credit and advertising, more leisure time, and the introduction of new gadgets, the 1950s ushered in an era of affluence that in some ways resembled the free-spending 1920s, but was to prove much more durable. The automobile came to play an ever greater role in American life, encouraged by the cheap price of gasoline and fueled also by the Eisenhower administration's policy of spending huge amounts on highway construction. This gleaming Pontiac Parisienne hardtop on display at the New York Coliseum auto show in December 1957 (left), with an equally glittering model in a tiara and strapless dress, epitomizes the glamour of the new consumerism. With unprecedented spending power, the young were also able to indulge their taste for sweet extravagance (above, an inviting soda fountain in 1958).

The Way We Were?

The 1950s are often seen as an ideal from which we have declined: Children were happy, families were strong, the economy was growing, and despite the fear of nuclear Armageddon, the United States was the greatest country—politically and morally—in the world. This Nebraska family settling down to watch *The Ed Sullivan Show* in December 1958 (above) encapsulates the domestic ideal. By 1960, 87 percent of American homes contained at least one TV, which came to play a major role in the construction of cultural and social values. *General Electric Theater*, which followed *The Ed Sullivan Show* on CBS on Sunday nights, was hosted by Ronald Reagan (right), whose folksy introductions to the dramas made him a household name and gave him the platform he needed for his later political career. But these happy days, which were in

many ways a reaction to the peculiar stresses of the Great Depression and World War II, and were underpinned by an international economic climate very favorable to the U.S., could not last. When the socioeconomic context changed in the 1960s, a more individualistic and libertarian ethos, more in line with trends earlier in the century, replaced the cozy domestic consensus associated with the 1950s.

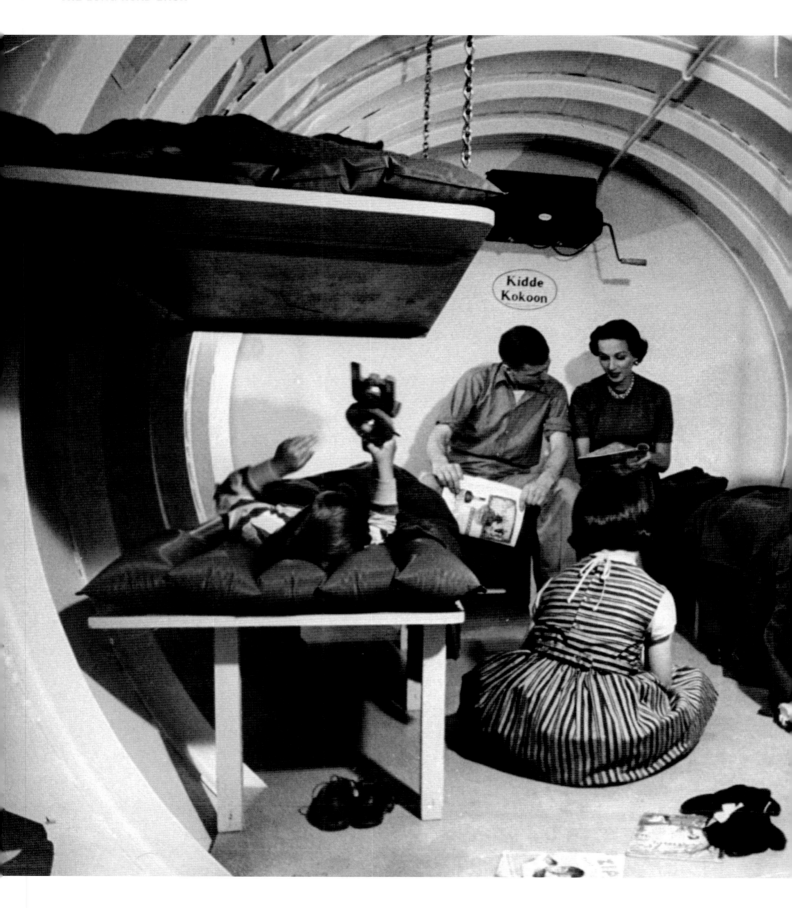

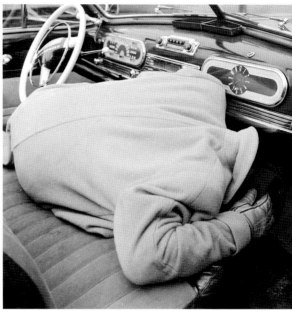

Nuclear Armageddon

The nuclear arms race created anxiety among ordinary Americans. Schoolchildren were drilled in how to respond to a nuclear attack, and bomb shelters were built in the gardens of some suburban homes, providing a daily reminder of the new threat. The powerful craving to maintain the domestic ideal under all circumstances is clearly visible in this 1955 government propaganda photograph of a family in a nuclear fallout shelter (left). As for the practical effect of the maneuver demonstrated (above) for taking shelter if caught in a car by a nuclear attack, it was surely a blessing it was never put to the test! Although his administration contributed to the buildup of the arms race, Eisenhower himself was uncomfortable about a policy that was premised on the Americans and Soviets being prepared to annihilate each other—the aptly named acronym MAD (Mutual Assured Destruction).

The Second Reconstruction

All his instincts told President Eisenhower to avoid confrontation, but when Arkansas Governor Orval Faubus barred nine black students from enrolling at Little Rock High School, as the 1954 Supreme Court ruling entitled them to do, Ike's hands-off policy was tested to the limits. In front of the world's media, a jeering, brick-throwing white mob set upon the nine students, unhindered by the police. Reluctantly, the president sent in the 101st Airborne Division paratroopers and placed the National Guard under federal control. White protesters were kept at bay (above) while the law was enforced. The national Democratic leadership—so dependent on the segregationist vote—was equally reluctant to grasp the racial nettle. A white policeman threatens blacks refusing to budge when refused service at a diner in Oklahoma 1957 (above right), and Dr. Martin Luther King Jr. is dragged off to jail in Montgomery, Alabama, in 1958 (below right).

The Rise of Anti-Americanism

Fury at U.S. support for repressive right-wing regimes was visited on Vice President Richard Nixon during what he optimistically termed a "goodwill" visit to South America in 1958. The tour was an unmitigated disaster. In Argentina, Nixon argued with protesters (top left), and in Caracas, Venezuela, his limousine was stoned by an angry mob (above and right). President Eisenhower had to order a detachment of U.S. marines from Honduras to protect the vice presidential party. Nixon was later to turn the episode to his advantage, and supportive journalists wrote glowingly of his courage in the face of an attempt on his life.

Kitchens and Corn

On a visit to the American National Exhibition in Moscow in 1959, Vice President Nixon and Soviet leader Nikita Khrushchev got into a heated ideological debate while viewing the latest gadgets in a model American kitchen—Khrushchev declaring that Soviet consumer goods lasted longer, so they did not need replacing all the time. A few months later Krushchev visited the U.S. and, in genial mood, made the most of every photo opportunity, such as the one (above) on an Iowa farm.

Secretary of State Dulles arrives at 10 Downing Street (left) on August 2, 1956, for a showdown with the British prime minister and the French president. Britain and France had sent troops to prevent President Nasser of Egypt from nationalizing the Suez Canal. The move was fiercely condemned by Eisenhower and the American government used the United Nations to block the Anglo-French action. But the U.S. was itself playing an increasingly interventionist role in the world. In 1958 marines landed on the beaches of Lebanon (below left) to support the pro-American government that was being assailed by rebels. The Department of Defense described the intervention as "like war but not war." U.S. military bases spread throughout the world as part of the administration's effort to contain Communism. When a security agreement was reached with

Japan, it provoked violent protests in Tokyo among young Japanese who feared that U.S. military bases would be established there (right). Ironically, the U.S. found it harder to control events in the troubled island of Cuba, only ninety miles off the Florida coast. For many years Americans had shaped Cuban development whenever they could, but in 1959 the charismatic revolutionary Fidel Castro (below right, meeting Vice President Nixon) seized power from the corrupt Batista regime. Castro immediately instituted a program of radical social improvement, but he antagonized the U.S. by attacking American commercial interests. As relations with the U.S. soured, Castro turned to Communism and the repression of political opponents. His regime was targeted repeatedly by the CIA, but to no avail.

The Campaign Trail

Nixon easily won the GOP presidential nomination in 1960 (below left) and set off in a hurry to stump the country (above left). With the Democrats nominating a New England liberal, Nixon spent far more time campaigning in Dixie than had any previous Republican presidential candidate (above, in Memphis, Tennessee), laying the groundwork for the "Southern strategy" that was to bear fruit eight years later. In a TV studio before one of their televised debates (right), Nixon and JFK square off for what was to become one of the most fiercely contested of all presidential elections.

Liberals in Danger

New York is a city that plays by its own rules, and New York Republicans have often been outside the national mainstream. Fiorello H. LaGuardia, who led a huge public works program, relaxes with a good cigar in 1945 (opposite, top left). Perennial liberal presidential contender Nelson Rockefeller has a quiet word with George Clyde of Ohio in 1959 (opposite, top right). Veteran liberal senators Jacob Javits and Kenneth Keating wave to the crowds in 1964 (opposite, bottom left). Activist mayor John V. Lindsay (opposite, bottom right, leading a cleanup campaign in 1967) later defected to the Democrats as the GOP moved more to the Right. An unresponsive group of Republicans listening to Rockefeller in 1959 (above) indicates that this brand of liberal Republicanism did not always travel well.

The Rise of the Right

The new Republican Right captured the presidential nomination for Barry Goldwater in 1964 and celebrated with a shower of gold coins (above left). The conservatives played on a widespread disappointment with the Eisenhower years for not having reversed Communism abroad or the New Deal at home. Goldwater faced a challenge from the wealthy liberal New Yorker, Nelson Rockefeller (far left, campaigning in the California primary), and from Pennsylvania governor Bill Scranton, also the scion of an old establishment family. Scranton's campaign was characterized by the cheesy slogans thought up by his supporters, such as "If Anyone Can Fill the Bill, Scranton Will!" and "Draft Bill Scranton? Sure We Will!" as well as by witty posters (left) that boasted of his liberal political views.

"Lyndon's War"

The war in Vietnam destroyed the presidency of Lyndon Johnson and with it the liberal dreams of the 1960s. A family awaits the safe return of a soldier from Vietnam in 1965 (left). Others were not so lucky (right). The loss of life contributed to the rising antiwar protests, including the Women's Peace Parade led by Jeanette Rankin, still alive and still fighting for progressive causes (below). As this pro-war march in New York in 1965 shows (below right), the Vietnam conflict was vehemently divisive.

A Second Act in Politics

While serving as a corporate ambassador for General Electric in the 1950s, appearing at functions across America, Ronald Reagan eased his way into politics, making sentimental, anti–big government speeches, harking back to an idealized America of a bygone era. In 1964 he made a TV appearance for Goldwater, which confirmed that, as his acting career wound down, he was bound for political heights. Reagan announced his candidacy for governor of California in 1966 (above) and won with a campaign full of razzmatazz (right). By the time of the 1968 convention (top) he had established himself as a leading and hugely popular GOP figure.

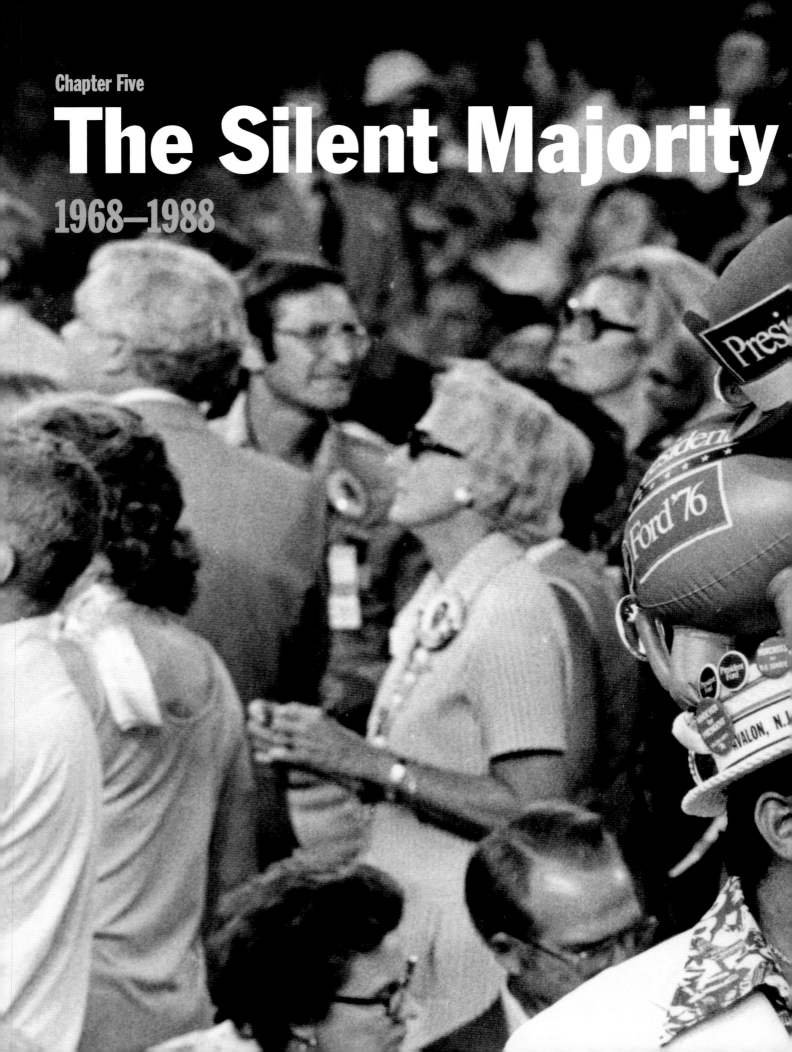

Chapter Five

The Silent Majority

1968—1988

The Silent Majority
1968–1988

I F ANY MOMENT IN MODERN AMERICAN history deserves the overused epithet "turning point," it is surely 1968, that momentous, emotionally charged year in which the dreams and nightmares unleashed by the 1960s rose to a crescendo. The assassinations of Robert Kennedy and Martin Luther King Jr. changed America perhaps even more profoundly than the death of John F. Kennedy five years before because the stakes seemed so much higher. Whereas the death of the president in 1963 had led to an increased commitment to achieve what he had been unable to do, the killings of 1968 made people fearful for the immediate future of the nation.

Richard Nixon understood the shock of these events and he knew how to reach out to those millions of Americans who had never been on a march or smoked marijuana, but whose television screens were filled nightly with images that seemed to suggest that the social fabric of American life was being pulled apart: hippies, black power salutes, protesters waving banners supporting the Vietcong. In a time of intense insecurity and anxiety about the future and about what America had somehow become, Nixon offered stability, reassurance, and an end to the seemingly permanent social revolution.

"As we look at America," Nixon told the delegates at the Republican National Convention in Miami in August 1968, "we see cities enveloped in smoke and flame. We hear sirens in the night. We see Americans hating each other, killing each other at home. And as we see and hear these things, millions of Americans cry out in anger: 'Did we come all this way for this?' " He promised that he would speak "for another voice . . . a quiet voice. . . . It is the voice of the great majority of Americans, the forgotten Americans, the nonshouters, the nondemonstrators . . . those who do not break the law, people who pay their taxes and go to work, who send their children to school, who go to their churches . . . people who love this country [and] cry out . . . 'that is enough, let's get some new leadership.' "

In Nixon, Republicans found a way to reconnect with the people. What Nixon was later to call the "Silent Majority"—and has often been known since as "Middle America"—began to emerge in 1968.

Nixon supporters at the 1968 Republican convention (above). Nixon captured the nomination ahead of the liberal Nelson

Previous pages: Delegates at the 1976 Republican convention, held in Kansas City, Missouri.

To Americans who feared the new permissive society's assault on traditional family values and notions of respectability and authority, Nixon offered himself as a man who had lived the American dream by raising himself from humble beginnings and as a firm defender of morality, true patriotism, and social order.

This was the year in which the New Deal order finally collapsed. Over the next twenty years the Republicans won five out of six presidential elections, and the only exception was in the wake of the Watergate scandal. Republicans found constituencies that had long been lost to them: white Southerners, blue-collar workers, union members, and even Catholics and Jews.

A key element in Nixon's victory was the success of what his aides called his "Southern strategy." With the former segregationist leader Strom Thurmond at his side, Nixon made carefully pitched appeals that swung the South behind him. This was a natural alignment. Nixon's appeal to "the forgotten Americans" was bound to appeal to the insecurities of white Southerners who had voted Democratic in the past only because their grandfathers fought for the Confederacy.

Nixon was not the only one playing this tune. George Wallace personified white resistance to the civil rights revolution, vowing in his inaugural address as governor of Alabama in 1963 to "toss the gauntlet before the feet of tyranny," and enforce "segregation today, segregation tomorrow, and segregation forever." In 1968 Wallace ran as an independent candidate and was even less restrained than Nixon in the way he tapped into the resentment against social protest. "If any demonstrator lays down in front of my car," he warned, exuding venom, "it will be the last car he ever lays down in front of." Wallace benefited Nixon's campaign by destroying the last vestiges of Southern white support for the Democratic Party. In the once-solid South the Democratic candidate, the hapless New Deal liberal Hubert Humphrey, who had loyally supported Johnson's war in Vietnam, won only 30 percent of the vote in the 1968 election, with much of his support coming from blacks.

The backlash against the civil rights revolution in Northern cities as well as in the South benefited Nixon directly. Republicans painted liberals as "elitists" whose concern for giving special privileges to blacks demonstrated their indifference to average (white) Americans. This subtle playing of the race card was only part of a broader onslaught on liberalism by this new, confident "conservative

Rockefeller, whose supporters tagged him "Rocky" in an attempt to make this man of inherited millions seem more like a man of the people (below). Nixon was swept to the White House with the aid of the segregationist George Wallace (left), who drew votes from Democrats in the South.

populism." Nixon's running mate, Spiro Agnew, blamed all society's ills, from drug abuse and sexual permissiveness to crime in the streets, on liberals. Echoing red-baiting Senator Joseph McCarthy and George Wallace, Agnew attacked intellectuals as "an effete corps of impudent snobs" who had "brought on a permissiveness that in turn has resulted in a shockingly warped sense of values." When asked what could be done about the poverty in American cities, Agnew replied, "When you've seen one slum you've seen them all." With this kind of language, Republicans spoke up for the ordinary folk against the liberal elites who were concerned only with the (largely black) underclass. Race and class, as ever, were closely intertwined.

Democrats also accused Republicans of using racist code when they focused on "law and order"—and indeed there was a loose association between race and the rising fear of crime—but crime mattered to ordinary Americans on its own terms as well. Liberal opposition to the death penalty was yet another example, Republicans charged, of the lack of understanding liberal elites had for ordinary Americans. In the eyes of Middle America, liberals were opposed to the traditional core values of patriotism, family, community, and tough law enforcement. In a breathtaking transformation, the experience of the 1960s created the perception that liberalism no longer represented the values and aspirations of the little man but was instead a somewhat abstract, self-indulgent set of commitments of relevance only to the well educated and the young. So comprehensively were the ideological foundations of the New Deal discredited that many Democrats eventually shied away from the "L-word."

The simple brilliance of Nixon's campaign in 1968 was to offer a reassuring promise of stability in a complex world of bewildering change and polarizing extremes. He did not alienate moderates as Wallace did because he was not threatening to roll back the landmark civil rights gains of the 1960s, but nor did he want to push racial change too hard. He did not want to abolish the welfare state, but neither did he want to extend it to those who were undeserving of public support. He was the candidate of containment.

The Republican victory, when it came, was an agonizingly narrow one—as is often the case with elections that change the direction of the country so fundamentally. Nixon polled 43.4 percent of the popular vote against Humphrey's 42.7 percent, with 13.5 percent for Wallace. Over the coming years, the Republicans built on this base to become the dominant political force in the nation.

President and Mrs. Nixon enjoying a stroll at the Great Wall of China on their historic visit in 1972.

The 1968 election foreshadowed the pattern of future political contests in another way as well: Only three out of five eligible voters bothered to cast a ballot. One poll showed that 43 percent of Americans disliked all three candidates equally. Ironically, in the first presidential election in which most black Southerners were able to freely exercise the franchise, the nation began its long retreat from active participation in electoral politics.

Richard Nixon possessed one of the most fascinating and complex personalities ever observed in American politics. On occasion he could appear poised and reflective, instinctively able to reach out beyond his core constituency and to understand his opponents' viewpoints. He could also be vindictive and petty, tormented by the thought that the elites he so despised looked down on him. He cared deeply about his place in history and the long-term implications of what he said and did. At the same time, he became obsessed with details, spending valuable time drafting long memos on such matters as when the White House curtains should be open and closed.

Nixon's presidency, like his personality, contained some curious paradoxes. Although some of his rhetoric was borrowed from Goldwater-style small-government thinking, he did very little to cut back welfare. This reflected the nature of the populist conservatism on which he had built his election victory. The middle class remained attached to the many welfare entitlements that benefited them. There was to be no return to some mythical pre–New Deal era of small government, despite the rhetoric and the hopes of conservative publicists. Confronted by a Democratic House of Representatives, Nixon was happy to sign into law bills that increased government regulation in areas like the environment. In August 1971 he even ordered a ninety-day freeze on prices and wages to curb inflation.

In the sphere of foreign policy, Nixon was at his most self-confident, negotiating breakthrough treaties with the Soviets that limited the superpowers' buildup of nuclear weapons. His visionary side was displayed most dramatically by his visit to China in 1972, a truly extraordinary reversal from a politician whose own rhetoric over the past twenty years had done much to build up the mutual hostility and lack of understanding between the two countries. Nixon's statesmanship in Beijing won him the unique accolade among modern political leaders of becoming the subject of an opera, *Nixon in China*. This iconic moment was the high point of his presidency.

One foreign policy issue that was not solved so easily was the war in Vietnam. In the 1968 election campaign, Nixon claimed he had a secret plan to end the war. The plan seemed to involve more bombing and the invasion of Cambodia. At home, antiwar protests became more and more intense, culminating on May 4, 1970, with the shooting by National Guardsmen of four student demonstrators at Kent State University in Ohio. This tragedy prompted massive protests on the Mall in Washington. A couple of days later the president, characteristically unable to sleep, crept out of the White House late at night and drove the few hundred yards to the Lincoln Memorial. He approached a group of astonished student protesters, stood awkwardly with them for a moment and then, instead of being able to find the words to reach out across a chasm of misunderstanding, made small talk about college football. In the bathos of that moment can be seen the insecurities that were to lead to his downfall.

Unsurprisingly, Nixon's life has often been portrayed as a Shakespearean tragedy in which the hero struggled against numerous setbacks and feelings of personal inferiority to achieve his highest ambition, only to see his dream disintegrate because of his own fatal weaknesses. Foremost among these failings was his willingness to abuse his office for domestic political gain, whether it was by compiling a list of domestic political foes to be harassed by the Internal Revenue Service, or, fatefully, authorizing and then covering up the break-in to Democratic Party headquarters in the Watergate Hotel during the 1972 election campaign.

Gerald Ford (right, in 1975) brought a much more open style to the White House after the Nixon years, but he failed to win the 1976 election.

Nixon would, of course, have won reelection easily in 1972 without resorting to burglary. The Democrats played into his hands by nominating the liberal George McGovern, and the Republican victory was a mirror image of the Democratic triumph in 1964, or even 1936, with Nixon winning all the electoral college votes except those of Massachusetts and the District of Columbia. Nixon was also able to offer Americans the prospect of "peace with honor" in Vietnam, negotiating a withdrawal of American troops. The eventual fall of South Vietnam did not occur until after a "decent interval," and by that time, Nixon was out of office.

Not long into Nixon's second term, the specter of the Watergate scandal began its steady drip of revelations that would lead eventually, on August 8, 1974, to the president's humiliating resignation, the first ever by an American president. The House was on the brink of impeaching him, and had it done so, Nixon had been warned by

Nixon (left, in 1971) was not dumped by the electorate as the Democrats wanted (above), but after winning a resounding victory in 1972, was forced to resign during his second term.

staunch loyalists like Senator Barry Goldwater that he could not even rely on Republicans in the Senate to support him. The sense of personal tragedy that hung over the departing president was palpable.

Nixon's successor, Gerald Ford, had been appointed vice president in 1973 to replace Spiro Agnew, who had been forced to resign over a corruption scandal from his earlier days in Maryland politics. "Our long national nightmare is over," the new president told the country. In a sense it was. Ford pardoned Nixon barely a month later, sparking charges that he was fulfilling his half of a corrupt bargain; but the resignation cleared the air. Nixon himself set off on his long journey to political rehabilitation.

The Watergate crisis did not, in the end, diminish Nixon's great political legacy: the new Republican majority. In 1976 the Georgia governor Jimmy Carter, an evangelical Christian who was conservative on social issues, won the White House campaigning as a Washington outsider. The weaknesses of his leadership, exposed by his unsure handling of the hostage crisis in Iran, paved the way for the return to power of the Republicans in 1980.

During the 1970s, a decade of economic crisis and high inflation, the Republican Party consolidated itself as the organ of populist conservatism. The old Eastern establishment, represented by men like multimillionaire Nelson Rockefeller, Ford's vice president, found themselves increasingly marginalized. In this decade, the mind and soul of the Republican Party was recaptured by an old orthodoxy: the nineteenth century–style free market with all the associated moral axioms of self-help and materialism. It was aided as well by the high-profile reentry into political life of evangelical Christians, who for decades had scorned involvement with the politics of this world, but who were now raising millions of dollars and supporting Republican candidates in a committed drive to redeem America from the moral crisis that had convulsed the nation since the 1960s.

Despite being a divorcé who was not in fact a practicing Christian, Ronald Reagan brilliantly captured the "family values" message, and his campaign in 1980 against a forlorn Carter became unstoppable. The Silent Majority was quiet no more. Unlike Nixon, Reagan was an old professional when it came to TV appearances and chitchat with the public. In the televised debates in the 1980 campaign, Reagan airily dismissed Carter's earnest and informed attacks on Republican policies with a twinkle and the folksy line, "There you go again!" For a while it became the nation's catchphrase. His sense of humor and self-deprecation made him impossible to dislike. When he was rushed to hospital after an assassination attempt in 1981, Americans chuckled with real affection at reports that when Nancy Reagan arrived at his bedside the president quipped, "Honey, I forgot to duck!" and that when he looked up at the doctors about to operate on him he joked, "Please tell me you're all Republicans."

Reagan, the former film star turned Republican politician, was not just good looks and charm. He had the knack of capturing the right mood and delivering his lines in a way that made people listen and trust him. Instinctively conservative, Reagan was also an irrepressible optimist whose pride in America and the American dream was simple and pure. And he could express that pride with affecting eloquence. For Reagan, the problems that America faced were the fault of leaders who were too obsessed with limits rather than possibilities. His role, once the voters had "rounded up a posse, sworn in this old sheriff, and sent us riding into town," was to restore national confidence. For him, politics was an uncomplicated business: Taxes and government were bad, the military was good; the purpose of foreign policy was to fight and defeat Communism. In office, Reagan behaved as if being president was not only enjoyable but pretty easy. That was not surprising, since he only worked on the nation's business for a few hours in the afternoon. An aide later recalled that, "Every word was scripted, every place where Reagan was expected to stand was chalked with toe marks." Just like the movies, in fact.

Large tax cuts were passed by a Republican Congress. As Reagan's budget director David Stockman admitted, this was simply the old Herbert Hoover "trickle-down" theory revisited. At the same time, Reagan called for, and received from a complaisant Congress, awesome increases in the military budget. The inevitable result was a budget deficit that would have appalled all previous generations of Republicans. It soared from $800 million when Carter left office to a truly staggering $1.4 trillion by 1984. This represented a failure of leadership for which Democrats on Capitol Hill share some of the blame. Ideologically committed to low taxes but unwilling to cut spending, especially the ballooning defense budget, the Reagan administration lived as if there were no tomorrow.

In 1980 Reagan had looked voters in the eye and asked them, "Are you better off now than you were four years ago?" By 1984 millions of Americans were confident that their lives had improved

Reagan's infectious smile and confident manner won over legions of "Reagan Democrats"—voters who had previously supported the party of the New Deal. They helped him to two massive election wins.

Republican Vermont congressman Jim Jeffords campaigning in 1981 among construction workers— traditionally seen as natural Democrats but now wooed as potential Reagan Democrats.

In 1984 Reagan was reelected by a landslide on the strength of national prosperity and his own uncanny ability to connect with the American electorate.

and that, after the long nightmare of Watergate and Vietnam, it was, in the words of Reagan's campaign ads, "Morning Again in America." Winning more votes than any other candidate in American history, Reagan utterly crushed the liberal Democratic challenge from Walter Mondale. The 1980s brought huge prosperity and rising incomes for a growing middle class, at least after the economy recovered from a business slump in 1982. There were more and more left behind, though. Cuts in welfare meant that tens of thousands of homeless people returned to the streets of American cities for the first time since the days of Herbert Hoover, half a century before.

Reagan had come into office calling the Soviet Union an "evil empire" and for four years refused to negotiate arms reductions. Then a Soviet leader appeared who challenged all the president's preconceptions. Mikhail Gorbachev's reforms, and the hopes for détente he raised among America's allies, eventually forced Reagan into a series of summit meetings. When the two leaders met in Reykjavik, Iceland, in 1986, Reagan alarmed his advisers by offering the Russians a deal to abolish all nuclear weapons. It was pure Hollywood fantasy, but as was the case with his fantastical "Star Wars" plan to build a "missile shield" to defend the United States, it revealed the president's deep yearning for a return to a gentler, safer age.

No president has ever been so detached from the details of the job as Ronald Reagan, yet few have been so effective at conveying their message. Reagan once spelled out his conviction that, "To grasp and hold a vision, to fix it in your senses, that is the very essence, I believe, of successful leadership." His vision was a simple one, and with his mind uncluttered by a raft of details or contrary arguments, he played his role with sincerity and conviction.

For the Republican Party, Reagan's legacy is the memory of a leader who projected back to them the image of America they most wanted to believe in. The party has rarely in history been as ascendant as it was in the mid-1980s. Republicans' confidence, expressed in their bumper sticker slogan, "We're Number One," was fully justified. Although Democrats still controlled the House, Nixon's vision of a natural Republican majority had finally come true. In this new post–New Deal world, rising social inequality was not a critical issue so long as the majority felt well off. In 1988, as the sheriff who had come to town to clean up a mess prepared to ride off into the sunset, the future had never looked brighter for Republicans.

The New Nixon

After a twenty-two-year career in national politics, full of setbacks and unlikely comebacks, Richard Nixon finally reached the White House. Pundits spoke of a "new Nixon" who had purged his demons and was determined to pursue a more moderate path as president. In a summer of great discontent and strong passions in America—Martin Luther King Jr. and Robert Kennedy assassinated, the war in Vietnam going badly, and racial violence consuming big cities—Nixon (top left) offered experience and stability. A go-go dancer at the Republican National Convention (left) shows commendable evenhandedness toward all the leading contenders for the nomination— George Romney of Michigan, Ronald Reagan, and Nelson Rockefeller, as well as Nixon—but this was Dick's year. Older women are in the crowd mobbing Pat Nixon on the campaign trail (above right). Older voters were indeed more likely to be Republican in the heady, youth-focused culture of the 1960s. But at least one group of younger female voters are definitely on Dick's side (right).

"A New National Majority"

Nixon (above, at the Republican National Convention, and right, with supporters during the 1968 campaign) appealed to Americans who were "un-black, un-poor, and un-young," in the words of political pundits Ben J. Wattenberg and Richard Scammon in their influential book *The Real Majority* (1970). Former Maryland governor

Spiro Agnew (above right, on the front cover of *Time* magazine in 1969) was Nixon's point man, ready to bluntly convey the administration's message, and, coming from a border state, the man who could best appeal to whites unhappy at Democratic civil rights legislation. Appealing to the "working men of this country," Agnew

described the 1970 midterm elections as a "contest between remnants of the discredited elite that dominated national policy for forty years and a new national majority, forged and led by the president of the United States."

INTRODUCING TIME'S BOARD OF ECONOMISTS
Prospects for Inflation and Recession

NOVEMBER 14, 1969

TIME

Agnew: Nixon's Other Voice

Reaching for the Stars

President Nixon in happy times and happy moods: fooling around with Sammy Davis Jr. onstage at the Republican National Convention in 1972 (left), in the White House with the pro-war Elvis Presley (opposite), and meeting the crew of *Apollo XI*, still quarantined after returning from their epic journey to the moon, on July 24, 1969 (above).

Now "Nixon's War"

With the aid of his national security adviser, Henry Kissinger, Nixon sought to end the Vietnam War by escalating it, including bombing raids on neutral Cambodia, through which the North Vietnamese forces transported supplies and reinforcements (above, Nixon explains the raids on TV on May 5, 1970). At the same time the president responded to the popular mood at home by announcing his policy of "Vietnamization"—the gradual replacement of U.S. ground troops with South Vietnamese forces. One of the factors behind

this gradual pullout were the images of decadence and indiscipline among U.S. troops broadcast on the nightly news (bottom left, a GI caught on camera smoking a joint in September 1969). The brutality of the war was brought home to Americans by the atrocities committed at My Lai in 1968, which only came to light later, in which 350 Vietnamese villagers, including women and children, were gunned down (above). The commander of the platoon that did the killing, Lieutenant William L. Calley, was court-martialed and sentenced to life imprisonment. But when a number of prominent conservatives, including George Wallace, called Calley a hero rather than a criminal, President Nixon made an exception to his tough law-and-order stance and commuted his sentence. Calley was paroled in 1974. The war also caused controversy for the use of chemical defoliants like Agent Orange (right), the use of which was stepped up under Nixon's presidency.

Peace Now!

Antiwar protesters were not all long-haired students burning draft cards (right). Vietnam veterans (above) and middle-class Americans too (left) were among those who took part in protest demonstrations, including one at Kent State University in Ohio on May 4, 1970, which led panicked National Guardsmen to shoot dead four students. Vice President Agnew blamed the victims, calling the deaths a "predictable and avoidable" product of the "politics of violence and confrontation."

Free World Leader

Richard Nixon considered himself very much a foreign policy president. In June 1974, just weeks before he was forced to resign, he visited the Middle East and is seen here (top left) with President Sadat of Egypt, waving from the train that took him from Cairo to Alexandria. No one could accuse Richard Nixon of being soft on Communism. And so he was in the ideal political position to formulate, with the help of Henry Kissinger, a new policy of détente toward the Soviet Union. He established a good working relationship with Leonid Brezhnev and agreed to a landmark treaty on limiting long-range nuclear missiles in Moscow in 1972 (above left). He visited the Berlin Wall in 1969 (left) and in 1972 normalized relations with Communist China, an astoundingly bold move that perhaps only he could have contemplated—and carried off with aplomb. Nixon is seen here with aging Chinese leader Mao Tse-tung (bottom left) and exchanging toasts with Premier Zhou Enlai (right).

When New York construction
workers attacked antiwar
demonstrators, the president
rushed to identify himself with
the "hard hat" protests (above,
at a Labor Day rally) and
brilliantly used antiwar
demonstrators as a foil for his
law-and-order rhetoric. "The
time has come to draw the
line," he said on the eve of
the 1972 election, "for the
great Silent Majority to stand
up and be counted against the

appeasement of the rock-throwers and obscenity-shouters in America." The GOP united behind Nixon (above, Ronald Reagan addressing the National convention). It was easy for the Nixon campaign (left, in Ohio) to paint his liberal, antiwar opponent George McGovern as the embodiment of everything that threatened American values. Nixon had one of the greatest of landslide victories (right, the ABC studio on election night).

The Darkest Hour

The Watergate scandal broke when James McCord (main picture), who was convicted of breaking into the Democratic headquarters in the Watergate Hotel, claimed that the White House knew of the burglary and had attempted to cover it up. In sensational testimony to the Senate Watergate Committee in June 1973, former presidential aide John Dean (top right) confirmed this and implicated Nixon directly. In April Nixon had fired two close aides, H. R. Haldeman and John Ehrlichman (below Dean, respectively), who, it later transpired, had acted on the president's instructions to smother an FBI investigation into the case. Other key figures implicated in this sordid tale included Attorney General John Mitchell (below Ehrlichman), who later served a prison term for conspiracy, perjury, and obstruction of justice, and E. Howard Hunt (bottom right), a member of the team of "plumbers" employed to stop government leaks—at any cost. Americans were stunned by revelations of a $400,000 secret fund to pay hush money and by the crude, dishonest, and desperate Nixon that finally emerged when the White House tapes were released—after nearly a year of stonewalling by the beleaguered president.

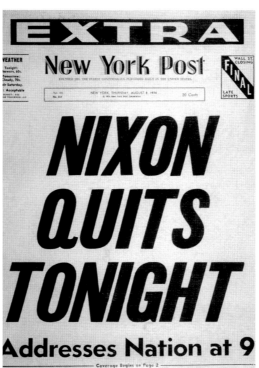

EXTRA

New York Post

NIXON QUITS TONIGHT

Addresses Nation at 9

The Last Act

Facing the humiliation of being removed from office by Congress, Nixon, who never admitted any guilt, resigned on August 9, 1974, the first president in American history to do so (above left, announcing his decision). Nixon turns away from the cameras after announcing his resignation (opposite), embraces his daughter Julie Nixon Eisenhower (left), and leaves the White House with a last, defiant wave the following day (above).

Busing in Boston

Social engineering was highly controversial during the early 1970s, and accelerated the drift in white working-class support toward the Republicans. A court-mandated plan to integrate public schools by forcibly busing children—sometimes many miles—in order to ensure a racial balance sparked violent confrontations in towns and cities across the nation. There were notorious disturbances in Boston in 1974. Police keep protesters at bay outside South Boston High School (below), while an escort is necessary to protect the convoy of buses as it arrives (left). Newly admitted black pupils celebrate for the benefit of the waiting media (right).

Peace of a Sort

Nixon had promised "peace with honor" in Vietnam. Talks in Paris (above) led to peace accords in 1973, which essentially agreed to a unilateral U.S. withdrawal in exchange for the return of American POWs held in North Vietnam (below, a POW is reunited with his family). In 1975 the discredited government of South Vietnam fell to the better organized and motivated North Vietnamese forces. Horrified American TV viewers watched the undignified scramble to get into the U.S. Embassy (left) in Saigon in order to get aboard the last American helicopter to leave the roof of the building before the city was overrun by Communist troops.

The Accidental President

For more than twenty years, Gerald R. Ford, a handsome former naval officer and college football star from Michigan, had served with distinction in the House of Representatives. But he had done so without ever gaining a high public profile. Then an unlikely series of events propelled this decent and honest man into the most powerful job in the world. In 1973 Nixon chose him to become vice president after Agnew was forced to resign on charges of corruption, and

a year later, when Nixon himself resigned, Ford became the only president never to have been chosen in a national election. His candid style was refreshing and did much to restore public faith in government (and in the Republican Party) after the Watergate scandal. He is seen here (above, left to right) being sworn in as president, on Air Force One, with British prime minister Harold Wilson in 1975, at

a cabinet meeting to discuss the fall of Saigon, and (below) in conversation in the Oval Office with Vice President Nelson Rockefeller and Secretary of State Henry Kissinger about the withdrawal of the last U.S. troops from Vietnam. But Ford's image was tarnished in the eyes of many Americans when he announced a presidential pardon for Richard Nixon. For Ford, the pardon was a means of

drawing a line under Watergate, the scandal that had done so much damage to the reputation of the GOP. As the president sorrowfully admitted, "If Lincoln were alive today, he'd be turning over in his grave."

A Perception of Decent Mediocrity

During a critical debate with Democratic candidate Jimmy Carter a month before the 1976 presidential election, President Ford (above, on the campaign trail, and opposite, waiting backstage before a campaign appearance) declared, "There is no Soviet domination of Eastern Europe, and there never will be under a Ford administration." It was a bizarre comment that fed a growing feeling in the media that this decent man was simply not up to the job. Ford, who chose Senator Bob Dole as his running mate (right), was unable to dissipate this impression and was duly defeated in a bland election.

Coming Apart at the Seams

Recession, in part caused by the spiraling price of oil and the rising problems of drugs and crime, contributed to the feeling that, in the wake of Watergate, America was in crisis. In 1979 the Iran crisis led to gasoline shortages (above) and the price of gas jumped to over a dollar a gallon. For the first time since before World War II, unemployment became a serious problem as the old heavy industries closed down. Unemployed autoworkers in Detroit lit fires to keep warm in the winter of 1979 (right) and lined up for welfare payments in July 1980 (above left). A drug raid in Manhattan in 1980 (bottom left). Against this background, Reagan's rhetorical question in a TV debate with Carter, "Are you better off today than you were four years ago?" was answered by many Americans with a resounding "No!"

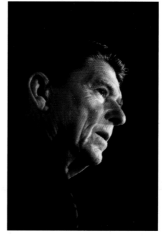

The Time Is Now

In the Republican primaries, candidate George H. W. Bush called Ronald Reagan's economic policy "voodoo economics," but when Reagan easily charmed his way to the nomination, Bush became a loyal running mate (left). The GOP slogan, "The time is now," captured the mood of determination felt by Republicans, who effectively capitalized on the mood of resentment and discontent in the country by offering fresh leadership and a new departure. The 1980 race was complicated by the presence of an independent candidate, John Anderson (right), a former GOP congressman who attracted support from a beleaguered band of liberal Republicans.

American Pride

Reagan's massive increase in the defense budget and his promise to "make America great again" endeared him to the armed forces. On a visit to the aircraft carrier *Constellation* in August 1981, the president salutes (above). Two years later in a bunker in Beirut, Lebanon, where a small American force had a peacekeeping role, a U.S. marine displays his loyalty to his commander in chief (left). To a degree unprecedented since the New Deal heyday of FDR, Ronald Reagan imposed his image, literally and figuratively, on 1980s America.

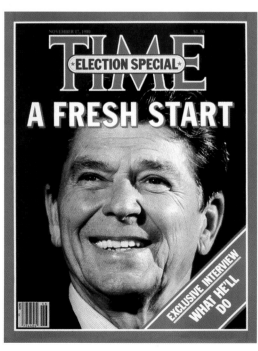

All Smiles for Reagan

The new president was geniality personified. Here he enjoys a laugh with, among others, Vice President Bush and Walter Cronkite (above), with Frank Sinatra and Nancy Reagan (right), and with congressmen (left) who had just presented him with a memento of his former life—a shirt advertisement from the 1940s. Few presidents have enjoyed their time in the White House as much as Reagan.

Assassination Attempt

On March 30, 1980, John Hinckley Jr. set out to win the heart of actress Jodie Foster, with whom he was obsessed. As the "greatest love offering in the history of the world," he tried to assassinate the president. Despite the close proximity of Secret Service agents and policemen, Hinckley got off six shots before he was overpowered (left), hitting Reagan under the left arm and seriously wounding him. The president is being pushed into the safety of the car (above). He was hospitalized for twelve days. At his trial in 1982, Hinckley was acquitted on grounds of insanity.

Rolling Back Communism

Reagan entered the White House determined to use renewed U.S. military strength to fight Communism wherever it appeared around the world, especially in America's "backyard" of Central America. In El Salvador the Reagan administration propped up a repressive dictator who used "death squads" to murder political opponents, and in 1983 U.S. forces invaded the tiny Caribbean island of Grenada, where a socialist government, friendly to Cuba's Fidel Castro, had taken power. Reagan holds crisis talks on the Grenada invasion with advisers, including Secretary of Defense Caspar Weinberger (right, standing), while a U.S. marine patrols next to a sign that sums up the aim of the mission (below right). Reagan's top priority, though, was to overthrow the left-wing Sandinista government in Nicaragua by providing massive military aid to Contra rebels, whom the president called "freedom fighters." The issue became a touchstone of toughness on Communism. White House communications director Pat Buchanan displays a T-shirt that quotes one of Reagan's more emphatic statements on this question (left), while protesters in California take an opposing stand (above left). In 1984 Congress refused to allow the CIA to provide military support to the Contras, but the administration would not be thwarted, sowing the seeds for what was to become the greatest crisis of Reagan's presidency.

Reaganomics

The theory was that sweeping tax cuts would stimulate the economy and total tax revenues would rise, eliminating the deficit while still allowing for a $1.2 trillion five-year defense buildup. The reality was that the tax cuts, financed in part by welfare cuts, led to huge budget deficits. Thanks in part to low worldwide energy costs, inflation remained under control and the economy grew steadily year by year from 1983 onward. But at 2.5 percent, the annual increase in GDP was actually lower than the 2.8 percent average during the bumpy 1970s. Reagan signs the 1981 tax bill (above right), celebrates the passage of the 1985 tax bill with a self-portrait (left), and waves a visual aid illustrating his tax reform proposals with New Jersey governor Thomas Kean in 1985 (above). At a reception for political cartoonists in 1987, Reagan chuckles at a caricature of himself backtracking on the tax cut issue (right).

Morning in America

The 1984 Republican convention (above and opposite) was an intoxicating celebration of the new sense of pride and confidence in America after the humiliations of the Vietnam and Watergate era. With the economy picking up after the 1981–82 recession, Reagan won reelection with more popular votes than any of his predecessors. His campaign theme, "It's Morning in America," was one of the most brilliant pieces of political advertising of all time, capturing the spirit of optimism that the president himself exuded. The conflation of fantasy and reality in the Reagan persona was summed up in his nickname, "the Gipper" (left), actually the name of a 1920s football star who Reagan had played in a 1940 film.

The Rise of the Religious Right

Back in the 1960s an evangelical minister named Jerry Falwell denounced any suggestion that Christians should sully their hands by interfering in the institutions of this world. "Nowhere are we told to reform the externals," Falwell argued, "the Gospel does not clean up the outside but rather regenerates the inside." Then came the countercultural movement of the 1960s and the Supreme Court's protection of a woman's right to have an abortion in *Roe v. Wade* in 1973. Falwell (right) together with Pat Robertson (below right) founded the Moral Majority in 1979 and made major inroads into the grassroots organization of the GOP, funding candidates who supported their positions and undermining those who did not. In a way this was a return to the Republican Party's evangelical roots, although now the prime target was sexual immorality rather than slavery. The Religious Right has had limited success in shaping legislation, but it has profoundly influenced American political culture more broadly, reintroducing the language of redemption and of "good" and "evil," and making an overt display of religious faith a near-obligatory requirement for ambitious politicians. In the 1980s the Religious Right suffered from the financial and sexual misdeeds of television evangelists such as Jim and Tammy Faye Bakker (above left) and Jimmy Swaggart (below left). Before being jailed for fraud, Jim and Tammy Faye managed to blow $60,000 on gold-plated bathroom fixtures, money raised from viewers of their Christian TV network. Although nothing to do with Falwell's Moral Majority, the scandals convinced many Americans that evangelical leaders were greedy and hypocritical.

The Iran-Contra Affair

"I don't remember," was Ronald Reagan's consistent and ultimately effective response to charges in 1986 that he had personally sanctioned the illegal sale of arms to Iran in return for the release of American hostages held by Islamic terrorist groups in Lebanon. The large profits generated from these sales were illegally diverted to the Contras in Nicaragua. Although the case had many similarities with Watergate, there was never any serious prospect of impeachment. The administration had covered its tracks too well. Admiral John Poindexter (left), national security adviser, was the principal fall guy—he was convicted of conspiracy, lying to Congress, defrauding the government, and destroying evidence. Marine lieutenant colonel Oliver North became a conservative icon for his brazen defense of his illegal actions during testimony to a congressional inquiry (opposite). Reagan was given an unusually difficult time by the press (above) but managed to remain, somehow, above the fray.

The New Gilded Age

Real estate tycoon Donald Trump
with his wife Ivana in their
palatial home in Florida in 1987,
their staff standing behind them.
When the marriage broke up,
Ivana became famous for the
zeal with which she pursued a
financial settlement with her
battle cry, "Don't get mad—get
everything!" During the 1980s
the top 1 percent of American
taxpayers controlled 40 percent
of the total wealth. To its
detractors, the unashamed
celebration of material excess
came to symbolize the Reagan
years. Trump tried to gain the
Republican nomination for the
New York mayoral campaign in
2001 but was defeated by
another multimillionaire, Michael
Bloomberg, who succeeded
fellow Republican Rudy Giuliani.

Victory Over the "Evil Empire"

In his first term Reagan refused to meet with the leaders of what he called the "evil empire"—the Soviet Union—and declared that the arms race was a struggle of "good versus evil, right against wrong." But then a new Soviet leader, Mikhail Gorbachev, emerged, who Reagan's close ally, British prime minister

Margaret Thatcher (below left), declared the West "could do business with." At their first summit in Geneva in 1985, Reagan and Gorbachev shake hands on the podium (above left). On a visit to Berlin in 1987, Reagan called on the new Soviet leader to "tear down this wall" (above). Just as Nixon had been able to stroll along the Great Wall of China safe in the knowledge that no one could accuse him of being soft on Communism, so Reagan, whose reputation as a cold war warrior was at least as secure, had the political leverage to visit Moscow and take a friendly walk with the Soviet leader in Red Square. Ironically, given the global threat that Republicans had always presented it as being, the collapse of the Soviet Union demonstrated its internal weakness.

Chapter Six

Brave New World

1988–2003

Brave New World
1988–2003

THE 1988 PRESIDENTIAL CAMPAIGN pitted a soft-spoken Ivy League graduate from a good New England family against the son of Greek immigrants who had worked his way up to be a popular state governor. It revealed much about how American politics had changed in the 1970s and 1980s that it was the wealthy Republican George Bush who was more successful at playing the part of man of the people, while his opponent, Michael Dukakis, appeared aloof and unsympathetic to the concerns of ordinary middle-income voters. For twenty years Republicans had won national elections where possible by portraying their Democratic opponents as elitists with no respect for traditional values. In this election it worked once again.

Nothing more effectively conveyed this Republican message than an infamous campaign ad that made Willie Horton a household name. Horton was a convicted murderer who, while on a weekend furlough authorized by Governor Dukakis as part of a program to rehabilitate offenders, murdered a man and raped his wife. Horton was black. Democrats immediately accused the Bush campaign of cynically playing the race card. The symbolism was certainly powerful; there is no stronger metaphor for racial hatred in America than a black rapist and a white victim, and a Republican consultant conceded that the blurred photo of Horton used in the ad was "every suburban mother's greatest fear." Republicans protested that this was exactly the kind of issue that revealed how out of touch liberal Democrats were with the values and anxieties of ordinary Americans. Both sides were right, but, in truth, Bush would almost certainly have won anyway.

With the economy apparently still relatively prosperous despite the stock market crash of 1987, Americans saw Bush, who for eight years had been a loyal vice president, as the man who would continue the Reagan policy of strong national defense. The world was changing fast. Bush had not been in the White House long before an extraordinary series of revolutions in Eastern Europe heralded the collapse of the old Soviet empire. By the time Bush left office in 1993, the USSR no longer existed. Republicans took the credit. There was perhaps a certain grim irony in the sudden collapse through internal

Soviet leader Mikhail Gorbachev appears open-handed in his approach to Soviet-American relations when meeting with President Ronald Reagan and President-elect George H. W. Bush in December 1988.

Previous pages: On Inauguration Day, 2001, ex-president George H. W. Bush relives his time in the Oval Office while his son George W. tries out his new chair for size.

weakness of a regime that, only a couple of years earlier, Republicans had been talking up as a growing threat to the free world. But it was undoubtedly the case that the inability of the USSR to compete with the extraordinary military expenditures of the Reagan years had been one of many factors that had weakened the regime. Optimistic talk of the "end of history" appears in retrospect to have been painfully naive, but it was certainly true that a great epoch of ideological confrontation between capitalism and Communism crumbled with the fall of the Berlin Wall. Republicans, many of whom for over forty years had been strident cold war warriors, were now entering a strange new world. If the enemy is gone, how do we know who our friends are? If our common foreign threat has been removed, what is there to maintain unity at home?

George Bush avoided the temptations of triumphalism to which many in his party succumbed. In 1991 his much-vaunted foreign policy expertise was tested by the invasion of the oil-producing Persian Gulf state of Kuwait by Iraq, which was governed by a neo-fascist dictator. Saddam Hussein had been showered with arms and aid by the West during the cold war, but was now, like Frankenstein's monster, turning on his creators by threatening the stability of this oil-rich region so crucial to American global interests.

Showing masterful diplomatic skills, Bush marshaled a huge military coalition under the auspices of the United Nations that successfully liberated Kuwait. This successful foreign war, resulting in remarkably few American casualties, expunged some of the memories of Vietnam, and in its aftermath Bush basked in some of the highest popularity ratings of any president in recent history. So impregnable did his position seem that several leading Democratic contenders decided to sit out the 1992 primaries. That left the field to a hitherto obscure Arkansas governor named Bill Clinton who, against all expectations, turned out to be the man who could puncture the apparent invincibility of the Republican Party.

Clinton described himself as a "New Democrat." Unlike Dukakis, he made a point of stressing his conservative credentials on "law and order" issues by flying back to Arkansas during the campaign to witness the execution of a mentally retarded black man who had been convicted of murder. He was also from the South, and with astonishing good luck for an American presidential candidate, he had been born poor in (or at least somewhat near) a town called Hope. He

The Bush-Quayle ticket won a comfortable victory in the 1988 White House campaign.

turned out to be a remarkably charismatic campaigner, and against George Bush, he was able to portray himself as someone who could speak to and for ordinary Americans. Bush's foreign policy successes appeared to have taken his eye off the domestic front, where recession was hitting hard. Famously, the Clinton campaign headquarters had a prominently displayed sign that read: "It's the economy, stupid!" It was this issue that proved to matter most in this first post–cold war election, and Clinton convinced Americans that he, rather than Bush, had the best plan for improving their well-being.

Clinton's victory came with the help of a third party challenge from Ross Perot, a multimillionaire who offered his business expertise as the solution to the nation's problems, and drew off many Republican votes. With less than half the electorate having voted for him, Clinton's presidency soon showed signs of political vulnerability. His entire eight years in office, which coincided with an almost unprecedented period of prosperity, became a continuing battle for the soul of America. On the one side was the generation that came of age in the 1960s, the "baby boomers" like Clinton, who had experimented with drugs (although Clinton claimed that he had "never inhaled") and dodged the Vietnam draft. On the other side were Republicans who, since Nixon, had been running against these very people. Now that the baby boomers had taken over the White House, traditional values seemed under threat as never before.

The Republican fight back produced a stunning victory in the midterm elections. In what its supporters hailed as the "Republican Revolution" of 1994, the GOP won a majority in both houses of Congress, and the new House Speaker, Newt Gingrich, became for a while the nation's most visible Republican. Gingrich, like Clinton, was a baby boomer who had avoided service in Vietnam, but in middle age the two came to personify each side in the continuing debate over the 1960s revolution. On all the touchstone issues of the moment— abortion, gays in the military, and whether government could solve social problems—Gingrich and Clinton disagreed. The triumphant Republicans issued a "Contract with America" that promised to end the budget deficit by cutting spending and to renew the public's faith in their political leaders. The president, though, was far too clever a politician to be easily wrong-footed, and the most remarkable thing about the Republican Congress that convened in 1995 is how quickly the momentum of their victory dissipated and how little political damage they inflicted on the president. When Republicans refused to

Secretary of State James Baker was Bush's campaign manager in 1988 and went on to play a leading role in the administration.

House Speaker Newt Gingrich heads for a showdown with President Clinton over the budget deficit in November 1995. Senate Majority Leader Bob Dole looks on thoughtfully.

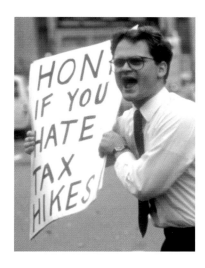

Bush's decision to raise taxes angered many traditional Republican supporters, including businessmen protesting outside the White House in 1992.

pass Clinton's budget in January 1996, the entire government was virtually forced to shut down. Federal employees could not be paid and welfare checks were stopped. Democrats were able to portray the Republicans responsible as callous and self-interested.

In the 1996 election, Clinton trounced Kansas senator Bob Dole, an old-style moderate Republican who had been Gerald Ford's running mate in 1976. Again, the election would have been closer had the irrepressible Ross Perot not thrown his hat into the ring, but even so, the 1996 election seemed to suggest that a new Democratic majority was at last emerging. Republicans were more than ever the party of the rural and suburban middle class and the party of corporate America, but Democratic strength in urban areas and among blacks and ethnic minorities seemed to give them the edge. The so-called Reagan Democrats—white, blue-collar workers who had defected to the GOP in the 1980s—were returning to their traditional allegiance. Republicans' conservatism on moral issues like abortion, prayer in public schools, and their steadfast opposition to gun control, made them appear intolerant and out of touch to a growing number of Americans. The perceived shrillness of the Religious Right alienated at least as many voters as it mobilized.

Every day that passed with Clinton in the White House was like a standing reproach to a growing number of conservatives on Capitol Hill, in well-funded think tanks, and in the media. No Democratic president since Franklin Roosevelt was so loathed by Republicans, a comparison that Clinton would undoubtedly appreciate, since what the two had in common was their conspicuous charm and ability to win elections that Republicans considered rightfully theirs. This animosity led directly to his impeachment.

Like the only previous impeachment—that of Andrew Johnson, another Southern Democrat who fell afoul of a Republican Congress—the issue that led to impeachment would have been ignored in other circumstances. Clinton was accused of having perjured himself by denying under oath that he had had a sexual relationship with an intern. Clinton's enemies saw impeachment as a means of ritually divesting him of some of the authority of his office, if not actually forcing him from office. In the midst of these extraordinary proceedings, the Democrats did well in the midterm elections of 1998. Recognizing that public opinion was not on their side, Senate Republicans in the end pulled back from the brink and decided that evading the truth over this kind of issue simply did not match up to the "high crimes and misdemeanors" stipulated in the Constitution as legitimate grounds for removing a president from office. Despite the earnest discussions among constitutional experts in the media, most ordinary Americans never really saw this peculiar episode as a great constitutional crisis. What they did see, nevertheless, was that Clinton had diminished his stature and that of his high office, and that his wriggling around the truth was a deplorable spectacle.

Although Republicans promised to cut taxes further than Democrats, the difference between the parties in the 1990s was as much about the moral and cultural values that each seemed to represent as it was over economic policy. Under Clinton, the budget was balanced and the national debt was reduced, although Republicans in Congress claimed—and deserved—some of the credit. The real lesson of the Clinton years was that the American electorate was evenly divided between the parties.

This point was dramatically proved by the extraordinary 2000 presidential election—a contest between Vice President Al Gore and Texas governor George W. Bush, the son of former president George H. W. Bush—which resulted, in effect, in a dead heat. In the nation as a whole, Gore clearly won more votes, but of course the American president is not elected by a nationwide popular vote. What counts is the popular vote in each state, and in several states the popular vote was so close that recounts were necessary. Eventually it all came down to Florida, whose electoral votes would decide who became the next president. All American elections have margins of error; never before had it mattered so much. The nation—and the outside world— watched mesmerized as the parties battled over what standards should be used to count the punch-card ballots that apparently worn-out, defective vote-counting machines had failed to read. The word "chad" entered everyday language. Other issues simmered just below the surface. As Democrats were quick to point out, the Republican governor of Florida, Jeb Bush, brother of George W., had been overzealous in his implementation of late nineteenth-century statutes that denied the suffrage to convicted felons. Blacks, nine out of ten of whom supported Gore, were, of course, disproportionately removed from the electoral register as a result. And so the wrangling went on.

More than a week after polling day, recounts were still going on in some Florida counties. As the days went by, what had begun as a farce became increasingly serious. Not since 1876 had the nation waited so

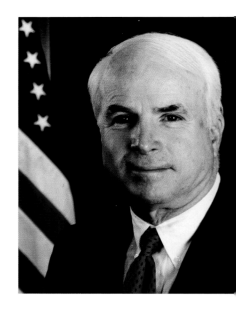

Arizona senator John McCain, held for several years as a prisoner of war in Vietnam, ran against Texas governor George W. Bush for the Republican nomination in 2000.

long for the outcome of an election to be decided. Tempers frayed. On one occasion, a gang of Republican activists physically prevented a recount from taking place. The sight of the world's greatest democracy being unable to make up its mind as to who it had elected provided foreigners—so often on the receiving end of lectures from Americans about democracy—with a field day. Fidel Castro offered to send over election monitors to resolve the dispute.

Homegrown satirists and other wags delighted in the confusion, but the impasse was revealing deep, underlying problems with the American political system. Although the electoral college was not due to meet for several more weeks, the Supreme Court, since the Reagan era an increasingly conservative body, was determined to take control of the process. In *Bush v. Gore* the Court ruled that the statewide recount that had been ordered by the Florida Supreme Court must stop; since there was, the Supreme Court asserted, no time to devise a means of conducting a recount that was fair, Bush had won because at the time when the Court metaphorically stopped the clock, he appeared to be marginally ahead in the popular vote.

The Court decision, which split along partisan lines, provided thin legal reasoning, and its assertion that its reasoning was "limited to the present circumstances" and should not be taken as precedent for any future cases seemed to Democrats to be evidence that the justices were aware of the thinness of their case. There were dark mutterings that the court had thwarted the electoral will of the American people and that the electoral college was a relic of eighteenth-century political conservatism, when the nation's Founding Fathers mistrusted direct democracy as a potential recipe for anarchy.

For Republicans, though, the right man won, and the system had proved itself. The Supreme Court's intervention was necessary rough justice, and it was time to put the arguments behind and get on with the business of government. By this reasoning, it was irrelevant that Bush had won a narrow technical victory in the courts or that Gore had won the popular vote by more than half a million, a margin greater than Kennedy's victory over Nixon in 1960. The second of the Bush dynasty to become president took office promising to work hard to earn the nation's respect, while at the same time acting as though he had a won a resounding "mandate." After eight years of watching a man they loathed enjoying power and popularity, the Republicans were back. Not only was their man in the White House, they also had control of both houses of Congress, albeit by narrow margins.

A Bush-Cheney bumper sticker from the 2000 election.

Unlike in 1877, when Republican president Rutherford B. Hayes took office after a very similar imbroglio, the Democrats did not make an issue of the president's legitimacy. This acquiescence is explicable because to have examined the structural failings that led to Bush's elevation to the highest office would have stirred up issues and conflicts that were too deep and too difficult. In any case, most Americans were accepting of the outcome. They understood that the basic situation was that the rules of the game, whatever the flaws in those rules might be, had produced no clear winner. The Democrats had no more credibility than the Republicans, because while they decried the partisanship of the Supreme Court, they could offer no alternative nonpartisan procedure for resolving the crisis.

Unlike his father, George W. Bush came into office with very little political experience. Yet his administration bristled with experienced old hands from his father's time, and from the Reagan, Ford, and even Nixon eras. In the first few months of the administration, the Republican Congress pushed through massive tax cuts for the most wealthy Americans and increased defense spending. Plans to exploit oil fields in Alaska and the decision to pull out of international treaties that committed the United States to cut down carbon dioxide emissions delighted the oil industry, which was well represented in Bush's administration, including at his cabinet table. Such actions dismayed environmentalists and provoked international protest. While he pursued a very traditional Republican economic policy, Bush had described himself in the election campaign as a "compassionate conservative," an apparent acknowledgment that after eight years of Clinton and the New Democrats, Republicans were in danger of being rebranded as the party of the wealthy elite, as they had been in the 1930s. It was in this spirit of inclusiveness that, although 90 percent of blacks had voted for Gore, Bush appointed the nation's first black secretary of state, Colin Powell, and another African American, Condoleezza Rice, as his national security adviser.

President Bush had not yet established a clear public image when the appalling terrorist attacks in New York and Washington on September 11, 2001, organized by a fundamentalist Islamic terror group known as al-Qaeda, changed the nation forever. From the moment the World Trade Center towers came down, nothing else in Bush's presidency mattered. The nation rallied behind him as Bush rose to the task required of him, providing a course of action that, he told Americans, would make their world a safer place once again.

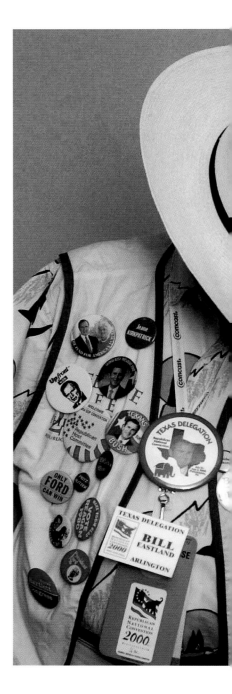

At a Christian Coalition rally in Philadelphia in August 2000, a Texas delegate proudly displays the spoils of thirty years of campaigning for the GOP.

Urged on by key advisers like Vice President Dick Cheney, who for several years had been advocating a more aggressive foreign policy, Bush chartered a new doctrine of the right of preemptive attack on any nation that the United States considered a potential enemy. Although the attacks of September 11 had generated an outpouring of goodwill from the rest of the world, the like of which Americans had not experienced since 1945, that support was quickly eroded by the determination of the Bush administration to act unilaterally.

In March 2003 Bush led the U.S. into a war against the Iraqi dictator Saddam Hussein without the support of the United Nations or any significant world power except Britain. Never before in its history had the United States embarked on a military adventure against the backdrop of so much international opposition. This single-minded unilateralism caused a historical reversal when most Europeans began to tell pollsters that they regarded the United States as the biggest threat to world security. At home, Americans continued to support their president, although for many with some unease. Nevertheless the speed and comparative ease with which the coalition brought down Saddam's regime was widely welcomed. America now bestrides the world, wielding a preponderance of military and economic power unseen since the Roman Empire was at its height. Yet the threats it faces are not from conventional armies but from alienated terrorists who resent the exercise of that power. Paradoxically, the United States's very strength may also be its Achilles' heel. Ultimately, Americans will judge Bush's foreign policy not on whether he wins friends or makes enemies abroad, but whether the Pax Americana he is trying to impose brings the dividend of increased security at home.

Meanwhile, Republicans continued to put their economic policy into practice. In March 2003 Congress passed a budget that sanctioned tax cuts for the wealthiest 15 percent of Americans and cut government spending sharply. The impact of the tax cuts on government revenue means that in the long term it may be hard to finance Medicare, Medicaid, and Social Security. Perhaps the Bush administration and its allies in Congress will therefore achieve where Reagan and the elder Bush failed and dismantle the remnants of the New Deal welfare state. If so, this may yet prove to be one of the most significant administrations in modern American history—and the United States that may emerge as a result may be closer to the Republican vision of how society should look than at any time since the 1920s.

Picking up Reagan's Mantle

The five candidates stake their case for the Republican nomination in 1988 in a TV debate (above, from left: George H. W. Bush, Pat Robertson, Jack Kemp, Pierre DuPont, Bob Dole). The eventual winner was Bush, scion of a quintessentially Eastern establishment family, who had previously been elected to public office in his own right only once. Despite having been Reagan's vice president for eight years, Bush was still a political mystery to many Americans. In a surprise choice, he tapped Senator Dan Quayle of Indiana (above right) as his running mate. Quayle immediately attracted controversy for his avoidance of military service in Vietnam, but his worst moment in the campaign came during the vice presidential TV debate, when he tried to draw a parallel between his own and President Kennedy's youth and relative inexperience for high office. Democratic candidate Lloyd Bentsen turned on him and witheringly retorted, "Senator, you're no Jack Kennedy." Bush, though, had the required political credibility. He and his wife, Barbara, wave to the crowd at a send-off for the U.S. Olympic team in September 1988. Still glowing in the endorsement of President Reagan, Bush and Quayle won an easy victory.

1989: Year of Revolution

In the months after George Bush came into office, the world changed forever. One after the other, Communist governments in Eastern Europe collapsed. In scenes that came to symbolize the end of the cold war, jubilant East Berliners climb over the wall that had divided the city since 1961 (top center). The following day, November 11, 1989, while a man hammers at the wall, from the other side East German border guards help the process, using water cannons that they had previously turned on protesters (right). In September 1990 former president Ronald Reagan—the man many credited with having helped to bring about the collapse of the "evil empire"— symbolically chipped away a remnant of the wall (top, far right). When Secretary of State James Baker visited Sofia, Bulgaria, in February 1990, crowds of well-wishers (left) hailed the American dream. But in Beijing, China, on June 5, 1989, this heroic pro-democracy protester stood alone to block the path of a column of tanks sent to end a student protest in Tiananmen Square (above). The protest was crushed.

"They are leaders who have made a difference.
Not because they wished it, but because they willed

-RN

The Nixon Legacy

President Bush, along with former presidents Reagan, Nixon, and Ford, poses amid statues of fellow statesmen of an earlier generation—including Churchill, de Gaulle, Khruschev, and Mao—at the official opening of the Nixon Library in California in 1990.

Desert Storm

When Iraq invaded Kuwait in 1991, President George H. W. Bush (above, speaking during a pre-war tour of European capitals) marshaled an impressive international coalition, secured the backing of the UN, and under the command of General "Stormin' Norman" Schwarzkopf (inset), U.S. forces led a successful military operation to repel Iraqi forces. The bow of the aircraft carrier USS *America* looms above the sand dunes along the Suez Canal on January 15, 1991, as it passes an Egyptian army truck and antiaircraft position (left). Retreating Iraqi forces torched oil wells, which required experts from the U.S. to extinguish the fires (below).

The Old and New Right

For many members of the Christian Coalition (above, at a 1996 national meeting), outlawing abortion, which they see as the legalized murder of children, is their number one political priority. In recent years, the pro-life lobby has been in the ascendant within the party, and since 1992 the Republican platform has included a plank favoring a constitutional amendment outlawing abortion, while leading Democrats have endorsed a woman's right to choose. But there is no clear-cut partisan divide. Many prominent Republican women are pro-choice and have been funded by a support group, founded by GOP fund-raiser Glenda

Greenwald (right) in 1992.

The problem for the GOP leadership is that while a majority of party activists oppose abortion, the electorate as a whole—especially the independent voters who need to be won over—are more moderate, and many are vociferously pro-choice (above right). The result is that despite Republican control of Congress, the White House, and the Supreme Court, no dramatic move to undermine *Roe v. Wade*, the landmark 1973 Supreme Court decision that legalized abortion, has so far been made.

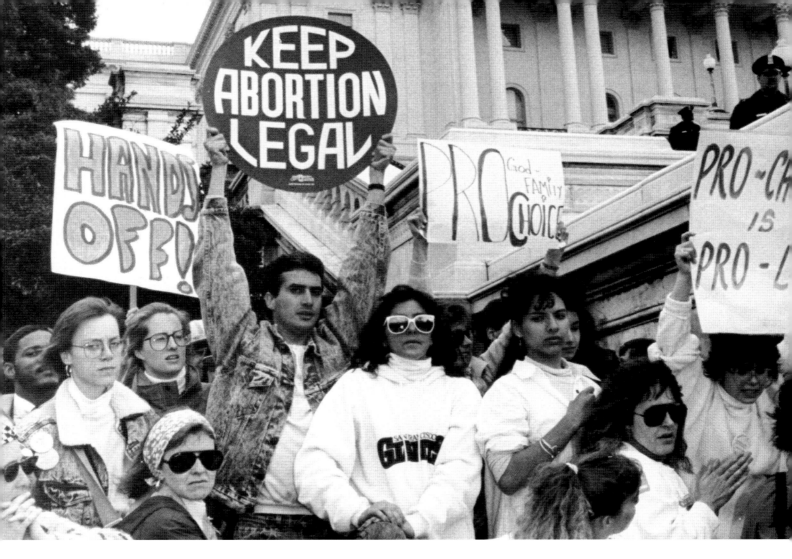

When former football star and sportscaster O. J. Simpson (below left) was arrested for murdering his estranged wife in 1994, it became the televised "trial of the century." When it was all over, surveys showed that by a three-to-one margin, whites believed that the predominantly black jury had exonerated a palpably guilty man. But by the same large margin, black Americans believed Simpson to be innocent. African Americans' faith in the impartiality of the justice system had been shattered by incidents like the beating of black motorist Rodney King by four policemen in the same city, Los Angeles, four years earlier. That incident attracted media attention because it was recorded on a passerby's video camera (above right), and because a white jury sided with the police, touching off riots in the black districts of L.A. In the face of this apparent racial divide, the GOP tried to improve its image with African Americans from within. Another black former football star, J. C. Watts (above left), congressman from Oklahoma, became a symbol of the new inclusive image of the party. Although only one in ten African Americans were Republican voters by the 1990s, George W. Bush reached out to racial minorities as part of his strategy of "compassionate conservatism." The difficulty was that the party's focus on "law and order"—an understandable response to concerns about crime among the middle class—distanced the GOP from the concerns of blacks, many of whom still lived a different life from whites in America. In 2000 there were more young black men in prison than in college. And death row inmates were also disproportionately black. Simple crosses mark the graves of Texas prisoners who have died on death row (below right).

The Many Faces of the Christian Right

The Christian Coalition was founded in
1989 under the directorship of the brilliant
young political strategist Ralph Reed (above)
to forge a new relationship between
fundamentalist Christians and the GOP.
About a quarter of new members of the
House in 1994 were affiliated with
evangelical churches. But this number still
understated the importance of the
Christian Right to the GOP. In 1992 Pat
Buchanan (left) ran against President Bush
in the primaries, and was a catalyst for
conservatives who felt betrayed when Bush
went back on his 1988 election pledge
("Read my lips—no new taxes"). The 1990s
also saw the rise of more extreme Christian
right-wingers such as the former Grand
Wizard of the Ku Klux Klan, David Duke
(right), a Republican member of the
Louisiana state legislature who ran for
governor in 1991 and had presidential
ambitions for the following year. Duke was
widely condemned for his overt racism.

Feeling Their Pain

With approval ratings of over 90
percent after the success of the
Gulf War, President Bush looked
set for an easy reelection in
1992. But Arkansas governor Bill
Clinton realized that while Bush
was respected for his handling of
foreign policy, he was vulnerable
on domestic affairs. With the
motto "It's the economy,
stupid!" Clinton, who proved
himself to be a brilliant political
performer (right, during a
televised debate), convinced
Americans who were suffering
from an economic downturn that
he "felt their pain." The race
was complicated by a third party
candidate, millionaire Ross Perot
(behind Clinton), who drew votes
from both parties, but more from
disaffected Republicans, helping
Clinton into the White House
with 42 percent of the vote
(against 37 percent for Bush and
19 percent for Perot).

Republicans on the March

Clinton's first two years in office were characterized by a series of political blunders and failed initiatives. In the midterm elections of 1994, Republicans made spectacular gains, overturning decades of Democratic control of the House and increasing their majority in the Senate. Senate Leader Bob Dole celebrates (top left), as does newly elected Senator Bill Frist of Tennessee (center left), who defeated the Democratic incumbent. But the man most associated with the triumph was Newt Gingrich (bottom left, taking Clinton to task), who issued a "Contract with America" designed to "restore the bonds of trust between the people and their elected representatives." All Republican congressional incumbents and candidates paraded up the steps of the Capitol (right) to sign the contract, which promised term limits, more open government, and a blaze of legislative activity in the first hundred days of the new Republican Congress.

The Buchanan Challenge

Archconservative Pat Buchanan (above) aroused passionate support (left) when he ran in the 1996 Republican primaries. His was a crusade to return the party to its traditional isolationist roots—what he called an "America-first foreign policy and an America-first trade policy." Like small-town Republicans of the early twentieth century, he wanted the GOP to "look out for American workers" and to reign in the power of big corporations.

A Battle of Ideas—and Generations

Senator Bob Dole of Kansas was regarded as a conservative when Gerald Ford chose him as a running mate in 1976, but twenty years later he had become the voice of moderation in the party. People trusted Dole (he had a 62 percent approval rating at the start of the campaign, compared to 42 percent for Clinton), and he was widely respected for his long record of service to the party and to the country. He also had a very politically savvy wife in former cabinet secretary Elizabeth Dole (top right, with Dole at a campaign stop at Dwight Eisenhower's boyhood home in Abilene, Kansas). But at seventy-three he was the oldest man ever to run for president from a major party—in fact, his heroic World War II record may have been a disadvantage, since it reminded people of his age. He also faced the difficulty of having to move to the right in the primaries in order to win the nomination. After selecting Jack Kemp as his running mate, Dole pushed for tax reductions (right) that appeared to be out of character. He also suffered from the handicap experienced by all challengers in a

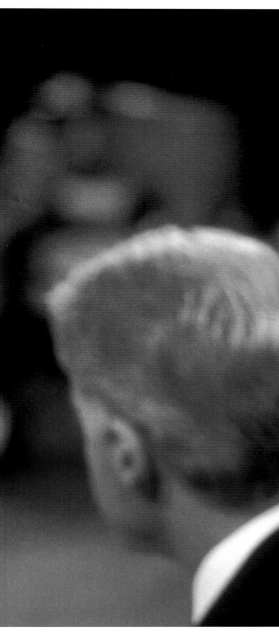

period of prosperity, and while the Dole campaign tried to paint Clinton as an old-style liberal, the Democrats had even more success in associating Dole with the unpopular Newt Gingrich. There was a problem in this election with the much-hyped "Republican Revolution," in that voters punished the Republicans as incumbents during the "revolution."

Impeachment of a President

One of the great political scandals of the twentieth century erupted in 1998 when President Clinton was accused of an affair with an intern, Monica Lewinsky (opposite, the two embrace at a Democratic fund-raiser on October 23, 1996). Clinton lied at a press conference (opposite, below) on January 26, 1998, with the line "I did not have sexual relations with that woman, Miss Lewinsky." From that point on the issue spiraled out of the president's control. Republicans in Congress seized on the issue. And a special prosecutor, Ken Starr (above), who had originally been appointed to investigate the Clintons' alleged misconduct on a property deal in Arkansas, turned his attention to whether or not the president had lied under oath while giving evidence on a previous case of sexual impropriety. With their majority in the House, Republicans were able to pass two articles of impeachment, indicting the president for perjury and obstruction of justice (above left, Chairman Henry Hyde of the House Judiciary Committee weighs the arguments). Democrats led by Dick Gephardt marched out of the House (left) on December 19, 1998, in protest against the Republican refusal to allow a vote on the lesser punishment of censure. Republicans in the Senate voted for acquittal.

Campaign 2000

Ralph Nader's Green Party campaign (above) energized many left-wing Democratic activists, drawing support away from Vice President Gore and helping the first son of a president to capture the White House since John Quincy Adams in 1824. George W. Bush fought a tough and bitter primary campaign against Senator John McCain (right, the two shake hands at the Republican National Convention). Texas delegate Carol Ryland holds up a placard expressing her support for the Texas governor (center right), and the candidate himself holds up three fingers to indicate three more days until the election at a rally in Dearborn, Michigan (far right).

The Florida Confusion

After the closest election in many years, all eyes turned to Florida, where recounts were still going on in selected counties. Both candidates needed Florida to win a majority in the electoral college and the presidency. The election seemingly descended into farce as the world become aware of hanging and dimpled chads—the tiny pieces of paper still clinging to punch-card ballots when the hole is not fully pushed through. Judge Robert Rosenberg of Broward County Canvassing Board tries to discern a voter's intentions (opposite, below left). Outraged by the exclusion of various categories of voters in Florida, a Democratic Uncle Sam demands justice (opposite, top). Meanwhile, a confident-looking Bush (left) is supported by New York governor George W. Pataki (opposite, bottom right). When the end came after five weeks of wrangling, Gore was tight-lipped in defeat.

Back in Power

True to his campaign image as a new kind of inclusive Republican, Bush appointed Colin Powell secretary of state—the most senior position ever held by an African American—and Condoleezza Rice as his national security adviser, the first woman ever to hold that post. During a White House meeting with Israeli Prime Minister Ariel Sharon on May 7, 2002, Powell gets a pat on the cheek from Rice (above). The president and vice president synchronize watches following the swearing-in ceremony for State Powell in the Oval Office (above right). On November 19, 2001, George Bush gets a surprise from a turkey called "Liberty" at the annual "Pardoning of the Turkey" ceremony in the Rose Garden at the White House (right).

The Day that Changed America

At a school in Florida, where he was
reading to the children, President
Bush is informed by his chief of staff,
Andrew Card, of the shocking attack
on the World Trade Center in New
York (right). The event came at a time
when the new president was under
fire politically, and had just lost control
of the Senate after the defection of
Republican Jim Jeffords. Now, normal
politics were suspended as Bush rose
to the challenge of his new role.

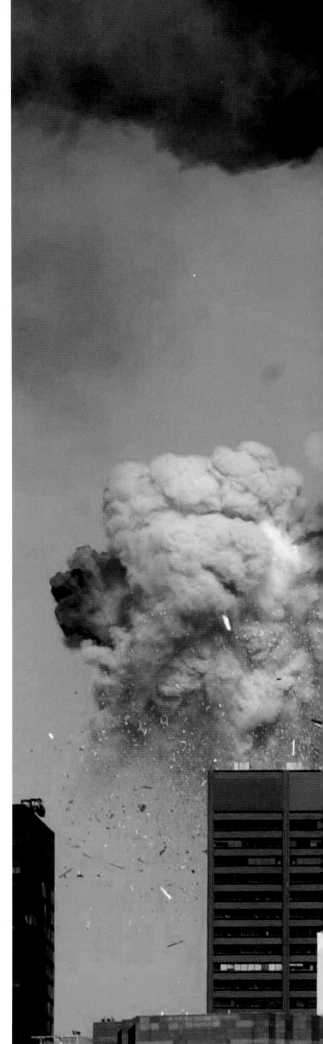

The War President

When President Bush addressed the American people about the terrorist attacks (above left), he denounced them as "acts of war" and vowed to bring the perpetrators to justice. Three days after the 9/11 attacks, he addressed firefighters, rescue workers, and police officers at Ground Zero (left). Republican New York mayor Rudy Giuliani inspired New Yorkers and the watching world as he worked tirelessly to set his shell-shocked city on the road to recovery. He is seen (above) with Governor George Pataki and Senator Hillary Clinton.

War on Terror

The Islamic fundamentalist Osama Bin Laden and his terrorist group al-Qaeda were suspected of conducting the attacks on September 11. The United States led an international coalition to overthrow the government of Afghanistan, which had been harboring Bin Laden. In the Tora Bora valley, troops take cover as they blast open a cave system in the vain pursuit of Bin Laden (opposite), the man who Bush said he wanted "dead or alive." America was in shock and support for President Bush and his war on terror was high and often pointed. Profits from the sale of this Wild West–type poster featuring Bin Laden (right) were donated to victims of the terrorist attacks. Many Americans were perplexed by the graphic evidence of anti-Americanism, especially in the Islamic world, that 9/11 unveiled. Demonstrators burn the American flag in Quetta, Pakistan (above).

Good Against Evil

For years, so-called foreign policy hawks in the Republican Party had been urging a unilateral exercise of American military power against "rogue states" like Iraq. Iraqi dictator Saddam Hussein (above left) waves a sword in defiance of the American threat of invasion. British prime minister Tony Blair gave staunch support to President Bush (above right), unlike some other European countries, including Germany, whose foreign minister, Joschka Fischer, listens skeptically to Secretary of State Colin Powell (opposite, top left). Germany, along with France, was dismissed as "Old Europe" by Secretary of Defense Donald Rumsfeld (opposite, top right, with Chairman of the Joint Chiefs of Staff Richard Myers). Demonstrators in Washington, D.C. (bottom right), oppose war in Iraq with a play on Bush's attack on the countries that make up the so-called axis of evil.

357

American Power

The invasion of Iraq went ahead without the support of the United Nations. Only Britain sent a substantial military contingent to fight alongside the U.S. Arab mistrust of American intentions in the Middle East was intensified by the campaign, but within three weeks, a vicious regime was destroyed. Refugees leave the southern Iraqi city of Basra (opposite, bottom) as oil fires burn in the distance; the capital city of Baghdad burns after repeated attacks from American bombers (above), and Iraqis wave to a column of U.S. tanks (opposite, top). All over Iraq, statues of Saddam Hussein were toppled (left), symbolizing the crumbling of a hated and feared regime. The military operation, though, may have been the easy part. President Bush promised Iraqis democracy, but ethnic, religious, and tribal divisions— not to mention reignited Islamic fundamentalism and opposition to the American presence—promised to make that transition a difficult one.

Outside the Texas State Capitol in Austin, thousands of supporters of George W. Bush celebrate the announcement of his election victory. The announcement proved premature, and they had to wait another five weeks before their candidate was safely confirmed. These are the kind of ordinary Americans who make the Republican Party—the party of freedom, of law and order, and of American patriotism—such a strong and enduring organization, one that has profoundly shaped the American past and will most certainly shape its future.

Editor's Note

The publication of this book has been a global effort, drawing on the expertise and knowledge of researchers and photographers within Getty Images and our partner agencies and many varied image sources. We at Getty Images are justly proud of our remarkable photographic collections. Our resources include Archive Photos in New York, which traces its lineage back to the oldest syndicated news agency in the United States, and FPG, whose stated aim was to champion the best in freelance photographers America had to offer.

In addition to Ali Khoja, who led all the picture research, we would like to thank Nicholas Webb and especially Mitch Blank at Getty Images in New York for their knowledge and expertise. In addition, our partners Time Life, whose archive, founded on Henry Luce's internationally renowned *Life* magazine, was made accessible through the help of Jeff Burak at Time Inc. As always, the Getty Images team in London, both at Hulton Archive and Getty Images News & Sport, made the myriad collections at the archive accessible. Particular thanks go to Matthew Butson, Brian Doherty, and Sarah McDonald at Hulton Archive. The majority of the contemporary material is drawn from the rapidly expanding Getty Images News division.

Beyond the Getty family we offer our thanks to:
Alison Lynn at the Republican National Committee, Karen Anson at the Franklin D. Roosevelt Library, Steve Branch at the Ronald Reagan Library, Nancy Mirshah at the Gerald R. Ford Library, Jessie Kratz at the Center for Legislative Archives, Andrea Felder and Tom Lisanti at the New York Public Library, Eleanor Gillers at the New York Historical Society, Piriya Vongkasemsiri at the Chicago Historical Society, Mari Artzner-Wolf at Ramsayer Research Library, McKinley Museum, Canton Ohio, Wallis Dailey at the Houghton Library, Harvard University, Lauren K. Glaettli at George Mason University, John Hallberg at the Institute for Regional Studies, North Dakota State University, Coi Drummond-Gehrig at the Western History/Genealogy Dept, Denver Public Library, Steven Williams at the Center for American History, the University of Texas at Austin, Ben Fathers at Agence France Presse and Martin Humphries at the Ronald Grant Archive.

CBM

Picture Acknowledgments

This book was produced by Getty Images Publishing Projects. We are grateful to the following sources for their kind assistance.

Chicago Historical Society Chicago Daily News Inc. 136-7, 137t, 137b, 142t, 142bl, 142br, 144t, 148; **Denver Public Library** Western History/ Genealogy Dept. 94l, 124-5; **Courtesy Gerald R. Ford Library** 206t; **Gamma** Charles Nye 272b; **Harvard University** Houghton Library, Theodore Roosevelt Collection 134; **Library of Congress** Prints and Photographs Division (LC-USZ62-98655) 16, (LC-USZC4-2569) 18-19, (LC-USZ62-36201) 20-1, (LC-DIG-cwpb-02960 DLC) 23b, (LC-USZ62-106337) Small, Maynard & Company 31, (LC-USZ62-110028) 33br, (LC-DIG-cwpb-03179) Samuel A. Cooley 36b, (LC-DIG-cwpb-02292) 37, (LC-DIG-cwpb-04294 DLC) 43, (LC-DIG-cwpb-02550 DLC) 44-5, (LC-DIG-cwpb-04166) 46b, (LC-DIG-cwpb-01786) Timothy H. O' Sullivan 47, (LC-USZ62-128709) Matthew Brady 48tr, (LC-DIG-cwpb-06437 DLC) 48br, LC-DIG-cwpb-04230 DLC)

Alexander Gardner 50br, (LC-DIG-cwpb-04202 DLC) 50tr, (LC-USZ62-1732 DLC) 58-9; Printed Ephemera Collection (Portfolio 173, Folder 25) 60-1, (Portfolio 205, Folder 27a) 74bl, (Portfolio 205, Folder 40e) 77b; (LC-USZ62-13018 DLC) 76t, (LC-USZ62-17168 DLC) Matthew Brady 84-5, (LC-USZ62-7607 DLC) 86r, (LC-USZC4-1813) Hugh Montgomery Hill 87b, (LC-USZ62-96156) 101t, (LC-USZ62-32953) 104-5, (LC-USZC4-3933) William Henry Jackson 108-9, (LC-USZ62-33590) From the U.S. Senate Collection, Washington Post Clifford K. Berryman 109b, (LC-USZ62-95067) 112b, (Digital ID 6a27399) Benjamin J Falk 114-15, (Digital ID 6a28277) Geo. R. Lawrence Co. 128-9, (LC-USZ62-95886) 133, (LC-USZ62-32737 DLC) George Grantham Bain Collection 138, (LC-USZ62-38780 DLC) 139t, (LC-USZ62-96172) 143, (LC-USZ62-128032) From the U.S. Senate Collection, Washington Post Clifford K. Berryman 147bl, (LC-USZ62-75334 DLC) 149t, (LC-USZ62-51323) Herbert E. French 164t, (LC-USZ62-98522) 165, (LC-USZ62-101984) 166l, (LC-USZ62-96154) 168l,

(LC-USZ62-110630 DLC) 170, (LC-USZ62-13829 DLC) 171t, (LC-USZC2-1085 DLC) Christopher DeNoon 177b, (LC-USZ62-84037) Rollin Kirby 178t (All Civil War photographs compiled by Hirst D. Milhollen and Donald H. Mugridge); **George Mason University Libraries** Special Collections and Archives, Oliver Atkins Collection Ollie Atkins 272t; **New York Historical Society** 22, 120bl; **New York Public Library, Astor, Lenox and Tilden Foundations** Photography Collection, Miriam and Ira D. Wallach Division of Art, Prints & Photographs (NYPG91-F104 019F)122r; Photographs & Prints Division, Schomburg Center for Research in Black Culture 72tl, D. C. Burnite 72tr, 81b, 90t; **North Dakota State University** Institute for Regional Studies, F. A. Pazandak Photograph Collection 126l; Milton R. Young Photograph Collection 126-7; **Courtesy Ronald Ronald Reagan Library** 203br, 301b; **Robert Hunt Library** Black Star Walt Sanders 196l, 197, Charles Moore 233b; **Ronald Grant Archives** 168r; **Courtesy Franklin D. Roosevelt Library**

187t; **McKinley Museum, Canton, OH** 118-19, 122l; **Topham Picturepoint** Associated Press 212, 213, Library of Congress (LC-USZ62-111014) 189tl **U.S. Senate Collection, Center for Legislative Archives** Washington Post/Clifford K. Berryman 147tl; **University of Texas at Austin** Center for American History, Robert Runyon Photograph Collection (08883) 161b, (08690) 162-3

All other images in this book are from Getty Images collections including the following which have further attributions

Agence France Presse J. David Ake 341tr, 341br; Robert F. Bukaty 353; Luke Frazza 356r; Ramzi Haider 359b; Mike Nelson 326-7; Paul J Richards 350tl; **Blank Archives** 124l, 176, 177t, 179b, 184t, 257t, 277br; **CBS Photo Archives** 214bl; **Consolidated News Pictures** Gene Forte 276; **George Eastman House** 152tr; P. F. Cooper 271; Lewis W. Hine 144bl, 144br, 145, 158, 159r; **Getty Images News and Sport** 229br, 348; Jim Bourg 344b, 345bl; Paula Bronstein 354t; CNN 322l, 331t; Karin Cooper 333l; Frank Fisher 282tl; Dirck Halstead 285, 288l, 342t; Geoff Hansen 336bl; INA 356l; Cynthia Johnson 336tl; Chuck Kennedy 343tl; David Hume Kennerly 357tr; Robert King 346bl, 346br; Steve Liss 289; Brad Markel 308b; David McNew 344-5; Mirrorpix 359t; National Archives 264; Matthew Nathons 297b; Per-Anders Pettersson 327br, 331b; Spencer Platt 358t, 350-1; James Pozarik 286t; Bill Pugliano 345r, 354b; Joe Raedle 316-17, 355, 358b, 360-1; Stacy Walsh Rosenstock 328t; Eric Smith 287; Anthony Suau 322-3b; Washington Times Ken Lambert 318-19, 330t, 343tr; White House Eric Draper 352b; Rick Wilking 347l; Mark Wilson 12-13b, 343b, 346t, 347tr, 349b, 352t; Alex Wong 357tl, 357b; **Bert Hardy** Front cover, 220-1, 222br; **J. Keppler** 62-3b; **Library of Congress** 8b, 9, 10-11, 17t, 21, 24-5, 25r, 26t, 28l, 28-9, 29r, 30t, 33bl, 34l, 34tr, 35, 38-9, 40t, 40b, 42t, 42b, 46t, 46m, 50l, 51, 52b, 53, 56-7, 58t, 62-3t, 68t, 68b, 70-1, 72bl, 72bm, 72br, 73, 74tl, 74r, 76-7, 78-9, 81t, 86tl, 88t, 88b, 90b, 91, 92tl, 92tr, 96b, 98, 101b, 107b, 110, 120br, 132, 139b, 141t, 141b, 152bl, 152br, 153tr, 153br, 154t, 154bl, 160-1, 164bl, 169, 172-3, 173r, 187b, 203t, 203bl, 232, 291tr, 316t; Alvin Langdon Coburn 1tm; Ralph Estem 156br; Alexander Gardner 1t, 49; Russell Lee 189tr; Timothy H. O' Sullivan 14-15; Nicholas Sheperd 18; Arthur Siegel 189b; Union Pacific Railroad Museum Coll./A. J. Russell 54-5; Washington Post/Clifford K. Berryman 111b, 164br; **Ken Love** 250-1; **Metropolitan Museum of Art, New York** From a painting by Thomas Hovenden 30b; **Jim Moore** 292b; **Museum of the City of New York** 152bm, 153bl; Byron Collection 87t, 102, 103t, 116l, 116-17, 135; Jacob A. Riis 96tl, 97, 106t; **Thomas Nast** 52t, 66-7, 96tr; **The Observer** Bryn Campbell 260t; Chris Smith 270bm; **Reuters** 322bl; Herbert Knosowski 322-3b; Win McNamee 342b; Lutz Schmidt 323tr; **Time Life Pictures** 188, 263tr, 265t, 270b, 330b; Michael Abramson 269t; Terry Ashe 256b, 258t, 259b, 304, 305b, 313b, 314-15; Ollie Atkins 12-13t; Black Star Sam Lafata 295r; James Nachtwey 292-3; Charles Bonnay 261t;

Larry Burrows 247tr; William F. Campbell 336ml; Ed Clark 206bl, 241b; Gordon Coster 201t; Ralph Crane 222bl; John Dominis 243br, 244tl, 245, 254-5, 271; Thomas S. England 302b; Nat Farbman 242, 243tr; Bill Fitzpatrick 297t, 298b; Gamma Michael Evans 291b; Ronald S. Haeberle 267l; Dirck Halstead 2-3, 281t, 282tr, 288tr, 291tl, 298t, 299t, 305t, 308t, 309, 312-13, 315t, 340-1; Acey Harper 333r; Kerry Hayes 329b; Image Works Stephen Jaffe 336-7; Carl Iwasaki 227r; Cynthia Johnson 296b, 314t, 320-1b; Yale Joel 210-11, 224t, 224b; Peter Jordan 290; Marty Katz 303b; Mark Kauffman 204, 205t, 205b; Robert W. Kelley 240t; David Hume Kennerly 282b, 283r, 284t; Steve Liss 258-9, 320-1t, 332, 338-9, 339r; Lee Lockwood 278t, 278-9, 279t; John Loengard 244br, 249; Mai 217, 310-11, 349t; March of Time 194b; Thomas D. McAvoy 179t, 208tr; Leonard McCombe 185t, 208br, 268; Will & Deni McIntyre 302t; Vernon Merritt III 248tl, 262-3; Mark Meyer 303t; Francis Miller 241t; Gjon Mili 274-5, 275t, 275tm, 275b; Ralph Morse 194t; Carl Mydans 222tl; Steve Northup 275m; A. Y. Owen 228-9; Lynn Pelham 260b; Bill Pierce 277tr, 300; Michael Rougier 238b; Walt Sanders 226-7, 230-1; Paul Schutzer 184-5, 234tl, 234bl, 235, 243bl; Arthur Schatz 6; Frank Scherschel 364; Robert Sherbow 329t; William C. Shrout 195, 198b, 243tl; George Silk 214tl; George Skadding 174-5, 219; W. Eugene Smith 180-1; Howard Sochurek 218, 236-7, 252b; Dick Swanson 266b, 267r; Allan Tannenbaum 327mr; Ted Thai 306-7; Patrick Tehan 296t; Grey Villet 211b; Diana Walker 1b, 292t, 299b, 321tr, 324-5, 327tr; Hank Walker 237r, 240t, 362-3; Julian Wasser 183b, 244bl, 248bl; Stan Wayman 246bl; Nik Wheeler 280-1; James Whitmore 209; Woodfin Camp John Ficara 301t, Ken Heyman 265b, Oliver Rebbot 284b; **University of Texas at Austin** Shel Hershorn 233t; **Tony Vaccaro** 215

For information about licensing Getty Images content contact your local Getty Images office

Life magazine photographer Francis "Nig" Miller (opposite) covering the 1956 GOP convention. He was a combat photographer for Naval Intelligence during World War II and joined the *Life* staff in 1947. What this photograph does not reveal is that Miller was an expert at concealed camera technique, deploying miniature cameras hidden under his tie, among other ruses. An excellent example of his work can be seen on page 241 (top).

Bert Hardy (below) joined the staff of *Picture Post* in 1941, and later during the war he served as an official war photographer for the British army. He was one of the first to enter the Belsen concentration camp when it was liberated in 1945. After the war Hardy returned to *Picture Post* and became almost legendary as Britain's premier photojournalist.

Previous pages:

Members of President Eisenhower's first cabinet in rapt attention as the president addresses the opening session of Congress on January 1, 1954. From left to right: John Foster Dulles, George M. Humphrey, Charles Erwin Wilson.

Index